# THE BATTLE OF ROANOKE ISLAND

# THE BATTLE OF ROANOKE ISLAND

*Burnside and the Fight for North Carolina*

MICHAEL P. ZATARGA

THE
History
PRESS

Published by The History Press
Charleston, SC 29403
www.historypress.net

Copyright © 2015 by Michael Zatarga
All rights reserved

First published 2015

Manufactured in the United States

ISBN 978.1.62619.901.9

Library of Congress Control Number: 2015932919

*For those who have had faith in me when even **I** had none in myself.*

# Contents

# CONTENTS

# Acknowledgements

Behind every written work there are dozens of people who aid the author in his craft. So it was with this work. It began with my family. Thank you to my parents, Michael and Patricia Zatarga, who fostered a keen sense of history and cultivated it with trips to battlefields and museums; to a maternal uncle, John Collopy, who taught me that history is not dates and figures but a story; and to his wife, my "Granty," who instilled a deep respect for the South and making a stand for what you believe in, even if in the end, you lose.

Thank you to friends past and present who encouraged me to write and who believed in me and my abilities. The names of these are too numerous to list, and pardon me if I forget to mention you here, but you know who you are; to the various members of reenactment units that I belonged to over the years who would ask me, "When are you going to write that book?" Thanks to the 150th Anniversary of the Battle of Hatteras Island Committee members who encouraged me to write the next stage in North Carolina's Civil War experience; to James Varner of Memphis, Tennessee, who offered some of his research materials for use in this book; to Dennis Schurr, who happily made his collection available for my use and taught me a valuable life lesson about looking at the objective in small segments rather than being overwhelmed by the large picture and for putting me in contact with The History Press; to the staff of the Fort Raleigh National Historic Site and its partnering Eastern National bookstore, especially Robin Davis, who provided editorial and writing encouragement through this process;

and to my commissioning editor, J. Banks Smither, and the good people at The History Press who so willingly published this work. Thank you to the staffs of various research facilities, including Jean Raintree of Brown University's John Hay Library; KaeLi Schurr, Dennis's wife, whose Outer Banks History Center staff in Manteo, North Carolina, is ever helpful and eager to aid; and the professional staffs of the National Archives at the Library of Congress and United States Military History Institute at Carlisle, Pennsylvania. A special thank-you goes to John Curran of the Peekskill Museum in Peekskill, New York, who always seemed to locate something new on my many research trips.

A writer is only as strong as his support group, and I am blessed with a great one. My wife and mother-in-law, Michaela and Joan McNamara, provided editorial revisions as well as an ear to listen to my various theories. Thanks to my children, Michaela, John and Brein—now you know why daddy took all those long car trips around Roanoke Island.

I thank you all.

# Introduction

Every year, nearly two million visitors come to the Outer Banks of North Carolina and Roanoke Island. They come for incredible beaches, venerable lighthouses, the site of the Wright brothers' first powered flight and the mystery of Sir Walter Raleigh's "Lost Colony," where England's first colonial attempt went horribly wrong. Visitors to Roanoke Island pass through the quiet areas of Manteo, not knowing what happened there 150 years before. The locals themselves seldom understand its importance as well. They pass the few roadside markers without any knowledge of their importance. Passing along the main road to the southern island village of Wanchese, hundreds of cars zoom through the very scene of the fighting. Along the roadside, in the shadow of a power substation, in an overgrown patch of grass bordered by a white picket fence, stands a small mound of dirt. The mound is not two feet high, and in front of the fence, a 1962 Centennial marker encased in brick briefly tells of the events on that February day. Fewer still know the importance of this spot. This is the last vestige of the three-gun battery where parts of eleven Union regiments tried to break the Confederate line for four hours. It was here that Captain Schemerhorn and his eighteen-pounder cannons held off two Union regiments until ammunition and determination failed, but it is more than a place where men fought.

The Civil War was fought in over one thousand places, ranging from St. Albans, Vermont, to the Territory of Arizona (today New Mexico). Over 660,000 men died in those conflicts, but here it was different. The war was in a critical phase. The Northern population had grown weary of the bloodletting; European powers intimated forced arbitration, thereby freeing the South, and all because of the lack of Northern battlefield victories. In early 1862, another failed battle for the North could mean the end of United States as one nation. For the North, success was no longer optional; it was obligatory.

In the South, political machinations had failed to pull off the expected European involvement, and as they prepared for the coming of the spring of 1862, their armies prepared for the Union attack waves to march southward. Limited resources meant difficult choices, and as such, some areas had to deal with less of everything. But who makes those decisions? A vital weakness in the Southern defense was illuminated here.

While the two sides battled it out, another group of people determined its own fate: African American slaves. A root cause of the war itself, slavery would be subtly affected by the actions at Roanoke Island. Slaves from coastal North Carolina waited to see which side would prevail. But while the vast majority merely witnessed the unfolding events, some abetted their own cause by offering Union forces their unique knowledge of the area.

Unlike most battles of the Civil War, the Battle of Roanoke Island was to have more far-ranging effects than simple casualties and exchanges of territory. The very fabric of the American nation would be transformed here. Warfare itself would undergo a transformation here, as the Union developed the techniques that would be used on one hundred battlefields in the twentieth century. Here at Roanoke Island, with the eyes of the world focused on the ensuing battle, the fate of the United States as a nation seemingly hung in the balance. Would the United States as a nation, like Raleigh's English Lost Colony, disappear or continue to transform into a new reality? The question would be answered among the sawgrass and swamp waters of Roanoke Island.

# 1

# Winter of Discontent

The sun had barely risen over a drab wintry Washington, D.C., on January 10, 1862, when a hunched-over Abraham Lincoln left the White House through a side exit. He was bundled against the damp weather with his usual top hat and a large overcoat that seemed to weigh down his already gaunt frame. He appeared older than his fifty-three years. It was as if the weight of the world was on his shoulders, and in the pre-dawn gray light, he shuffled along with only the leafless trees in the presidential park standing guard. He covered the distance to the War Department building, located just outside the gated park, with long strides. He was, as he routinely did, heading to the Telegraph Room on the eastern front of the building to find out the latest war news. As he approached the gray-clad buildings, there were no guards; the building would not be bustling with activity for another few hours. The only staff on duty this early was the telegraphers, busily scratching down the latest incoming transmissions and then tapping out the accepting notifications on their Morse keys. They didn't take time to notice as the frail-looking gentleman, coat and hat in hand, strode into the room. He would have told them to continue their work anyway. That was how President Abraham Lincoln was.

The physical weight on his shoulders lifted, Lincoln rifled through the latest in communiqués. It was the same. The winter weather had forced all military operations to a standstill. The emotional weight was still there. He heaved a sigh and continued to read. President Lincoln had much to be depressed about this winter.

Throughout the war, Abraham Lincoln suffered with three interrelated demons: battlefield defeats, war apathy and European recognition of the Confederacy. Each in their turn would rise and fall through the war's four years, and Lincoln found it a delicate balancing act to make sure these factors did not combine to overwhelm the Union's war effort. While these pressures would rise exponentially, individually, with the establishment of slave emancipation as a Union war aim in 1863, they would never be as high, in a combined sense, as they were in the winter of 1861–62.[1]

The summer had seen volunteers drawn to the military in huge numbers, but one after another, the armies suffered disastrous defeats. First was at Manassas in July 1861. Only twenty-five miles from Washington itself, the battle, which was distinctly heard in the capital, ended in an abysmal rout. The carnage that one Congressman had expected to wipe up with his own handkerchief turned into one of the nation's bloodiest battles. But more was to come. No sooner had the nation consumed the news of this battle than another calamity occurred.[2]

Only three weeks after the debacle at Manassas, Union Brigadier General Nathaniel Lyon attempted to wrestle Missouri from the Confederate forces. The battle was ferocious, and Lyon killed along with over 1,300 of his men, the remainder running northward, leaving Missouri a divided state. Confederate forces followed up their victory with an assault on Springfield, Missouri, in September. The ensuing siege left the Union with only a slight bridgehead centered on St. Louis. But there was still worse to come.[3]

In October, the new main Union army stationed in front of Washington itself attempted to flex its muscle. Ever since the defeat at Manassas in the summer, the Union army, now styled the "Army of the Potomac," had been training under its new commander, Major General George B. McClellan. McClellan had stationed his troops along the Potomac River north of Washington, and in the fall, he ordered his various troops to cross the river and raid the Confederates on the southern side.

On October 21, a brigade crossed the Potomac above Leesburg, Virginia, commanded by Lincoln's friend and former Oregon senator Edward Baker. In fact, Lincoln's second son, who had died in 1851, had been named after Baker. Baker's troops crossed in force at a place known locally as Ball's Bluff with only three leaky boats. The troops initially succeeded in establishing a crossing, but while the bluecoats were still crossing, the Confederate defenders arrived from Leesburg and set up a devastating counterattack. With blistering volleys, the Confederates drove Baker's Yankees back to the brink of the bluff. At this critical part of the battle, Baker was killed, and two of the boats foundered. With little chance of escape, the troops surrendered or attempted to swim the Potomac. This disaster was magnified not only by Baker's closeness to the president but also by the scene of dead Union soldiers being fished out of the Potomac River just a few miles from the White House the following week.[4]

The personal loss to the president was immeasurable. The First Family had to substitute for Baker's own wife and children at the viewing, as they were still in Oregon, and Lincoln was visibly moved to tears. The war had hit home to the very doorstep of the White House, yet this was not the only cause of Lincoln's melancholy.

General war numbness had settled over the Northern populace. Victories had eluded their armies, and the lists of the dead filled newspapers. Horace Greeley, the editor of the pro-Republican *New York Tribune*, described New York City in the late summer of 1861 as having

The mouthpiece of the Republican Party, Horace Greeley, the editor of the *New York Tribune*, represented the fears of the Northern populace. *From the Library of Congress.*

"on every brow sits sullen, scorching black despair."[5]

Some newspaper editors, Greeley among them, began to reiterate their belief that the South should just be allowed to leave the Union. Writing to Lincoln only days before the battle at Manassas in July, Greeley questioned:

> *Can the rebels be beaten after all that has occurred, and in view of the actual state of feeling caused by our late awful disaster?...And if they can not be beaten—if our recent disaster is fatal—do not fear to sacrifice yourself to the country. If the rebels are not to be beaten—if that is your judgment in view of all the light you can get—then every drop of blood*

*henceforth shed in this quarrel will be wantonly, wickedly shed, and the guilt will rest heavily on the soul of every promoter of the crime.*[6]

It was obvious who Greeley was holding responsible as the "guilty promoter." The very same editor who had coined the phrase "on to Richmond" only weeks before now held the president responsible for the needless deaths. He called for an armistice, an exchange of prisoners, the disbanding of the U.S. army and a national convention "with a view to a peaceful adjustment." With the added failures of the fall, the cries for a peace settlement became louder.[7]

With newspaper editors like Greeley calling for a reconciliation or disunion after this first summer, it is not hard to see a groundswell of popular peace support beginning to take effect. As stated before, the casualties were far beyond any the nation had suffered before or thought it would have suffered in what was supposed to be a summer-long conflict. Now, with the war grinding on, peace protestors began to spring up across the North. At first, protests were hidden in the rush of patriotism in the run-up to the battle of Manassas. Habeas corpus had been suspended in many of the border states, like Maryland, and in unsigned editorials, many argued against government infringement of this right. Then, protesters took to the streets as mothers and widows marched in some Northern cities decrying the wasted youth. The next step was men like Greeley publicly attacking the president, which would lead to a possible fifth column, or collaborators organizing against the federal government. Already a dangerous organization with potential fifth column intentions, the Knights of the Golden Circle, was known to be making inroads into the states of Indiana, Ohio and Lincoln's own Illinois, funneling money and medicines to a needy Confederacy. Some wondered what the next step might be—sabotage?[8]

But of course, all this could be alleviated with a large success on the battlefield. The armies, now asleep under their winter blankets, were large enough. It was not that the armies were or could not be fed or clothed but rather could they maintain their overwhelming numbers. After the summer defeats, the patriotic Northern states redoubled their efforts, and another 300,000 Union soldiers joined the seasoned campaigners to swell the ranks. But with the lack of victories on land, Lincoln was forced to turn to the navy to project Union power with a blockade. In the first year of the war, the blockade was more myth than practice, as the U.S. Navy, woefully inadequate before the war, had to increase its sailors and ships. Until the Navy grew larger, through a combination of commandeering existing ships and launching new ones, the blockade was extremely porous. Adding to their inability to stop Confederate commerce, the few naval incursions transporting Union army units were small and seemingly inconsequential.[9] But it was a naval action on November 8 that added a new realm to Lincoln's kingdom of discontent.

Up until November 8, the European powers, mainly France and England, had viewed the conflict from the sidelines. Both sides offered dichotomous aid with offers of peace arbitration as well as weapon supplies between the warring factions. Arbitration would be an admission of defeat for the Lincoln administration as, whatever the result, the South would succeed in leaving the United States. Therefore, arbitration was refused out of hand. It was also no secret that the Europeans viewed the United States as an economical threat to their empires. Northern industry was beginning to rival industrial giant Great Britain, and with raw materials located in the nearby South, the United States could produce items more cheaply than their European adversaries. But with a separate Southern nation, the Northern industry would fall behind the Europeans, and without Northern tariff constraints, Southern raw materials, especially cotton, would be available on European markets, driving down prices overall. Southern states would benefit greatly from European recognition, but African slavery was the key stumbling block.

In the early part of the century, a tide of Christian religious revival swept both France and Great Britain. As a result, both nations saw slavery as morally wrong and had abolished it in their colonial territories; Britain had taken it upon itself to destroy the slave bases in Africa, further crushing slavery at its very core. By 1860, slavery formally existed only in the Western Hemisphere, in the Portuguese colony of Brazil and the United States' South. Compelled by religious leaders in both countries, the European governments were forced to side with the North as the war took on greater and greater emancipatory importance. So, as of November 1861, the governments in Europe leaned on the South and the people leaned toward the North.[10]

Also on November 8, off the Bahamas, U.S. cruiser *San Jacinto*, acting on a tip that Confederate representatives James Mason and John Slidell were on the Royal Mail Ship *Trent* to petition for English aid to the Confederacy, intercepted the *Trent* in international waters. *San Jacinto* overhauled the British ship and removed the two men and their staffs. Immediately, the British filed protests that the men were under their protection and that the Union had committed an act of war. They demanded an apology and the representatives' immediate release.[11]

Confederate ambassadors Mason and Slidell come aboard the USS *San Jacinto*, beginning the Trent Affair. *From* Harper's Weekly, *November 30, 1861.*

Papers on both sides of the Atlantic printed bellicose saber rattling. Some in the North, including Secretary of State William H. Seward, believed that a foreign war would unite the United States far quicker than any political action and actually favored a war over the Trent Affair, as it was called. To prove his point, Seward pointed to the example of the War of 1812 in which southern soldiers fought beside northerners against the common enemy. But this was a different time and different issues. Most were realists and realized that a British intervention would be greeted in Richmond by cheers and not as a call to defend American territory.[12]

In the halls of the British Parliament, the arguments resounded. The North had violated the rules of war by attacking a neutral ship and in doing so had put British citizens in danger. It had challenged the British Empire. The North had unwittingly already confirmed nation-state status of the South by declaring a blockade on Southern ports. Only belligerent nations can be blockaded. Belligerent Britons insisted the British Empire should declare war on the North and aid the South, forcing arbitration on the former United States, for peace's sake. The North countered this combative feeling by stating that the South's departure was an insurrection and not an outright rebellion. The blockade was a quarantine of the Southern coastline to protect United States shipping. In response to the Trent Affair itself, the North questioned that if Mason and Slidell were insurrectionists (i.e., criminals) then why was the British government defending them? British newspapers soon began to call for John Bull's vaunted military to be employed in North America to box Uncle Sam's ears, beating his ragamuffin soldiers and leaky navy while Northern newspapers prepared the nation for a third war with Great Britain. In reaction to the growing alarm, Prime Minister Lord Palmerston ordered nearly ten thousand British soldiers to Canada to bolster British defenses in the North. War seemed inevitable.

At this point, the Queen interjected. As her representative, her husband, Prince Albert, began a marathon effort to ratchet down the war rhetoric. Though dying from pneumonia, Albert succeeded in calming down Palmerston's pro-Southern administration with reminders of the true underlying cause of the conflict: slavery. Realizing that siding with a slave state would be unpopular with the general public, Palmerston, through diplomatic channels, agreed to a compromise of a formal apology and the release of Mason and Slidell. The Lincoln administration, seeing the honorable exit left by Palmerston, assented to the repatriation of Mason and Slidell the day after Christmas but refused to apologize. Angered but with honor satisfied, both sides returned to normal relations. Unfortunately for the North, Prince Albert, the most vocal pro-North voice, died soon after, leaving relations tense.[13]

With defeat on the battlefield, war apathy and European intervention factoring in Lincoln's every war decision, it is hardly surprising that in the winter of 1861–62 he felt depressed. Discussing the daily affairs with Quartermaster General Montgomery Meigs later this day, January 10, Lincoln's depression openly manifested: "It is exceedingly discouraging. General, what shall I do? The people are impatient; Chase has no money and he tells me he can raise no more; the General of the Army has typhoid fever. The bottom is out of the tub."

Never again during the war was the question of the nation's survival so much in doubt. Victories in the West would offset losses in the East, war apathy would turn to resolution and the Europeans' own participation resolve would wane. But at this very instant, Lincoln was morose, and the question of the Union's survival was in doubt. "What shall I do?" he begged of Meigs.[14]

# "The Army Is Gathering from Far and from Near"

T he day before Lincoln's melancholy public outburst to a sympathetic Montgomery Meigs, the new campaign season officially began. At Annapolis, Maryland, nearly fifteen thousand Union soldiers waited dutifully in ranks to file onto eighty ships of various sizes and shapes. They clambered aboard steamships, sailing vessels and barges to the shouted commands of their sergeants. Stevedores and quartermasters argued on the placement of supplies, while horses whinnied in protest as they were slung aboard ships and placed in the dark holds. By midmorning, the fleet was ready to depart. Signal flags were hoisted and signal guns boomed as the ships powered up or set sail and began to push out into the nearby Severn River. Regimental bands competed with one another by playing patriotic tunes. Troops cheered and jibed one another as the heavily laden ships passed one another. Color sergeants uncased their colors and waved them gaily in the breezes. The colors and sounds seemed more appropriate to a cruise ship leaving port than a military expedition. The men cheered everything, and when the flagship, the smallest ship in this impromptu fleet, passed by to take the lead, they cheered it as well. The men had no idea where they were going, but after months of monotony, they were happy to be going anywhere. One of the few men who had knowledge of their ultimate destination was aboard that small ship. He was Brigadier General Ambrose Burnside.[15]

Ambrose Everett Burnside was a tall, brawny, robust but slightly paunchy figure. The "very beau ideal of a soldier," described one reporter, but at thirty-seven, Burnside was already mostly bald with hair plastered thinly about the sides.[16] What he lacked on his head was more than made up with a huge set of whiskers that ranged down his cheeks and met on his top lip. It was a fashion that he did not create but, by the end of the war, would forever be linked to his name: sideburns. He was a friendly, good-natured fellow and a hardworking individual, but fortune always seemed to fail him when he needed it most.

Rising from poverty in Liberty, Indiana, in the 1820s, Burnside struggled with money throughout his life. He had lost his mother in 1841, forcing him to work as an apprentice tailor before his schooling was finished. But, gifted with a keen business acumen, two years later, he had not only finished his apprenticeship but was also a minor shareholder of the business when he resigned from the lucrative position to accept an appointment to the U.S. Military Academy at West Point. There, he graduated a respectable eighteenth in a class of thirty-eight in 1847.[17]

Unfortunately, his military career began at the end of the Mexican War, and Burnside saw no action south of the border that graced other future Union generals' records. Instead, his service was split between the western frontier against the Apaches in the recently acquired Arizona Territory, where he was wounded in action, and garrison duties on the East Coast. A short stint as quartermaster for a survey team on the Mexican border earned him a promotion to first lieutenant in 1851. Returning east in the spring of 1852, Burnside married Mary Bishop Richmond in Providence, Rhode Island. With a new bride and the usual slow advancement in a peacetime army, Burnside needed a new outlet.

Ever the tinkerer, Burnside had spent his off-duty time perfecting a breech-loading rifled carbine design. Burnside's design relied on a hinged breach block mechanism that opened with the compression of the trigger guard as an operating lever. Exposing the breach block allowed the soldier to place a specially designed tapered brass cartridge in the block. Closing the trigger guard placed the block into position, and ignition was created by the hammer striking a brass cap filled with fulminated mercury. The carbine was solidly made and was a substantial improvement in hitting power and operator safety as the block's tight seal reduced compression gasses from escaping. The cartridge, also designed by Burnside, focused the black powder's energy, increasing the bullet's range and accuracy. Realizing its possibilities could make him rich, Burnside resigned from the army in the fall and, with money loaned by some friends, founded the Bristol Rifle Works. Dubbed the "Burnside Carbine," it worked well in trials and was favorably reviewed by government inspectors, but the Burnside Carbine lost an 1858 military contract when then secretary of war John B. Floyd requested a kickback. Burnside was horrified by this level of government graft and refused to pay, and the contract was rescinded. Without the contract, the Bristol Rifle Works was forced to declare bankruptcy, compelling Burnside to sell the design for his carbine. Burnside, nearly penniless, and his family were forced to move west, with creditors hounding his every move.

At his lowest ebb, Burnside appealed to a former West Point classmate and dear friend George B. McClellan. McClellan, the vice-president of the Illinois Central Railroad, offered his downtrodden friend a position as cashier of the railroad's subsidiary land company and opened his house to the Burnside family in the spring of 1858. Employed and living with McClellan allowed Burnside to pay down most of his debt, and in June 1860, he was promoted to treasurer of the railroad, with offices in New York City. It was there that Burnside learned of the start of the Civil War.

Three days after Fort Sumter was bombarded by the new Confederate army, President Lincoln called for seventy-five thousand militia to suppress the rebellion. Burnside—a West Point graduate and a former major general in the Rhode Island militia from his days in Providence—was soon tapped by Rhode Island's governor, William Sprague. A trained officer was a valuable commodity at that time, and Sprague wired Burnside with an offer to command Rhode Island's first militia regiment. Burnside agreed and was soon placed in command of a brigade of four regiments in the Union army assembling outside Washington, D.C., in June 1861.

Burnside proved capable enough to command troops, and while the battle at Manassas might have been a Union debacle, Burnside's brigade handled its first battle with sufficient pluck to rout its Confederate adversaries early in the battle. With few Union champions, Burnside's limited victory on such a depressing day soon elevated him to hero status in the Union army.[18] Better tidings for Burnside came the day after the fight when his old friend McClellan, fresh from a minor success in western Virginia, was appointed as the new commander of the Union army.

In early September, McClellan proposed to the War Department the formation of a "coast division" whose immediate goal was "for operations in the inlets of the Chesapeake bay and the Potomac. By enabling me [McClellan] thus to land troops at points where they are needed, this force can also be used in conjunction with a naval force operating against points on the sea-coast." This division was to consist of two brigades of five regiments each from New England, because the men there were supposed to be most familiar with "boat service to manage steamers,

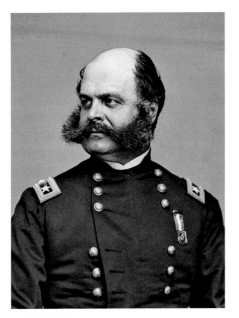

Born of humble circumstances, Burnside was a likeable, stalwart solider. Here, he sports a Ninth Corps badge, which germinated from his "Coast Division." *From the Library of Congress.*

sailing vessels, launches, barges, surf-boats, floating batteries etc.," which the division would employ continuously. Troops would carry specially made waterproofed cartridge weapons and fight with small naval howitzers, called Dahlgren boat guns, attached to each regiment. Ships would be purchased or chartered to carry the division on its expeditions, manned by detached soldiers from the division itself and run by the army. McClellan was adamant that the troops were part of his newly christened Army of the Potomac and not just another ad hoc naval assault. As a portion of his army, McClellan determined that the "coast division to be commanded by a general officer of my selection." With a well-placed friend and popular support, Burnside's star rose sharply, and on September 12, McClellan tapped his old friend for the command. McClellan expected the division to ready in a month's time.[19]

Unfortunately, McClellan's permission to organize the division ran into several obstacles. Burnside's recruitment ran afoul of two similar expeditions being organized at the same time. The bulbous Massachusetts politician turned general Benjamin Butler had been looking to remove the stain of losing the first land battle at Bethel in June 1861 as soon as the troops had returned from that skirmish; now he had his sights set on attacking the North Carolina coast at Hatteras Inlet. He had the troops garrisoning in Newport News and Fort Monroe on the Virginia Peninsula but needed naval support. He finally crowded two regiments and some artillery onto two small transports and, with a fleet of three warships, sailed south in August 1861, drawing first blood with his victory there on the twenty-eighth.[20]

The other expedition was headed by newly appointed General Thomas Sherman, also from Rhode Island. Not to be seen playing favorites,

McClellan refused requests from both Sherman and Burnside for troops from the Army of the Potomac. Without this manpower pool to draw from, both expeditions were sent scurrying, canvassing northern governors for newly formed regiments. Sherman won the race for more regiments, and his expedition completed organization first, setting sail in October, leaving Burnside to contend with those regiments not chosen. They were not exactly what Burnside desired.[21]

On October 21, the day that Sherman's expedition sailed from Annapolis, Maryland, bound for Port Royal, South Carolina, Burnside and his first recruits arrived at the sleepy colonial Maryland village along the Severn River. Burnside's first regiment, the Eighth Connecticut, disembarked from its troop trains and moved into Sherman's recently deserted camps while they were still being emptied. The Eighth Connecticut was just the kind of regiment Burnside was not interested in. It was composed of farmers and merchants from the north-central portion of the Nutmeg State. Flooding to enlist in droves, hundreds Connecticut men descended on Hartford, Connecticut, in August, filling up the Eighth Connecticut to recruitment strength in less than a month. They did this with a blind eye toward the recruitment regulations, as several fair-skinned African Americans were sprinkled through the rank, even if the law forbade "coloreds" from serving with white soldiers. Few of the Connecticut men were seafarers, but while in their camp of instruction on Long Island, New York, Burnside liked what he saw in the Eighth's military bearing and quickly got their orders marked for Annapolis. They were commanded by Edward Harland, a Yale-graduated lawyer who had already seen combat at Manassas in a ninety-day regiment. He was tough disciplinarian and a thorough tactician.[22]

Burnside's next regiment arrived nine days later from New York. The Fifty-first New York Infantry was commanded by a former Italian dance master from New York City, Edward Ferrero. He was considered an expert in dance, penned a how-to book and even taught dance class to round out officer cadets at the nearby U.S. military academy at West Point. Wealthy, Ferrero paid for the Fifty-first's needs from his own pocket. He was also a well-connected New York politico and, for six years, a lieutenant colonel in the New York militia. He was ably seconded by another attorney turned soldier, Robert Potter. But for many of Ferrero's men, from New York City, Brooklyn and the surrounding communities, the only water service they had been on were the various ferries that carried people to and from New York City.[23]

November saw the arrival of several regiments from Massachusetts to Annapolis. The Twenty-fifth Massachusetts Infantry arrived on the third

A strange dichotomy: the military dance master, Edward Ferrero (left), and the aggressive lawyer, Robert Potter. *From the Library of Congress.*

and encamped next to the Fifty-first New York. The Twenty-fifth was headed by Colonel Edwin Upton, a lumber merchant with twenty-five years' experience in the militia and salt-and-pepper hair that did not reflect his true age. Born in 1815, Upton was old enough to be a grandfather to many of his men, but his sturdy frame described a stalwart soldier. The Twenty-fifth was recruited from western Massachusetts in the foothills of the White and Green Mountains, which made it another strange choice for a coastal division.[24]

The Tenth Connecticut arrived the next day clothed in gray overcoats against the wintery weather. The Tenth's colonel, Charles L. Russell, was only thirty-three but had already reputation for drill and instruction, although he was also known as a caring officer, traits not usually found in equal amounts in officers. The Tenth and the Eighth had more than a shared familiarity. Colonel Russell had recruited a company for the Eighth, but when offered the lieutenant colonelcy for the Tenth, he demanded that his company follow him as well. A company of the Tenth was then traded to the Eighth for Russell and his men. This friendship was rekindled when the Tenth encamped, and both

Well-liked Connecticut drillmaster Charles L. Russell. *From the Outer Banks Historical Society, Manteo, North Carolina.*

Connecticut regiments held joint officer trainings schools at night and drill sessions during the day while they waited for orders.[25]

On the fifth, the Twenty-seventh Massachusetts arrived and soon joined the ever growing camp outside Annapolis. The Twenty-seventh was commanded by the former city clerk of Springfield, Massachusetts, Horace C. Lee. Lee, a balding man with the bookish look of a clerk, had originally been assigned to the Twenty-first Massachusetts, but when Governor John Andrew needed experienced officers to command five new regiments in the late summer, Lee was immediately tapped. His men, like Upton's Twenty-fifth, were recruited from Western Massachusetts, but when ordered to the front, Lee's men marched overland to the Hudson River and took boats nearly eighty miles to New York City instead of the more common route of marching southward to rail lines in Connecticut to transit to New York and points farther south. They had been sailing for the better part of week when they arrived at the Annapolis docks, having sailed from New York City. Many of the landlocked Bay Staters were still green from the experience.[26] A week and a half later, on the fourteenth, Burnside's sixth regiment arrived, marching with its lead company, wearing distinctive blue- and red-trimmed jackets and trousers. The men were, like all the other soldiers in Annapolis, chatty and excited to be involved in some operation, but the colonel, John Kurtz, was not. Kurtz, wearing a bushy shortened beard, was disgruntled by the idea of a seaborne operation. He had expected to be with the main army, but with his usual self-possession, Kurtz never let his disappointment interfere with his regiment's training. Soon the regiment was drilling daily, and by the end of the December, the men were honed to a razor's edge with the men marching, drilling and looking (the distinctive uniforms having been packed up and sent home) like a well-oiled machine.[27]

Pennsylvania's only contribution to the expedition had a history far longer than its regimental number might suggest. It began on the road to Manassas. The majority of regiments that composed the Union army in July 1861 were recruited for what many thought would be the duration of the war: ninety days. Contract-minded soldiers kept daily tabs as the time passed and they panted for a battle, but the Fourth Pennsylvania was not among those engaged. Shunted from one Union army in the Shenandoah Valley to the one in front of Washington, the Fourth Pennsylvania was quickly closing in on its muster-out day when the main Union army pushed on to engage the Confederates. Its expiration date, July 20, 1861, was one day shy of the battle at Manassas itself. Union commander Irvin McDowell personally implored with them to stay, but the Pennsylvanians would not be moved, and as the rest of the army moved toward the battlefield, they marched back to Washington, D.C. McDowell unfairly laid some of the blame for the ensuing Manassas rout on shoulders of the retiring militiamen. Arriving home after the news of the battle reached the local newspapers, the men were shunned for not having actually served under fire. In an effort to redeem their reputations, the regiment reenlisted under their former colonel, John F. Hartranft, a Norristown lawyer with a steely gaze. The Fourth Pennsylvania reentered the service as the Fifty-first Pennsylvania Volunteer Infantry. There would be no turning back for the Fifty-first this time.[28]

The very same day the redemption-seeking Fifty-first Pennsylvania arrived, Burnside's most colorful regiment—in all variants of the word—the Fifty-third New York Infantry, marched in. Dressed in a imitation of the colorful French colonial/African troops known as the Zouaves, the Fifty-third wore red fezzes with yellow tassels, blue short jackets with yellow trim and short, baggy light blue trousers with white canvass leggings covering their shoes. The uniform was supposed to be an emulation of the famed Sixth Regiment of the Imperial French Guard. It was commanded by a seventeen-year veteran of the French army, Lionel Jobert D'Epineuil.[29] It had several French officers commanding the companies and seemed to have that rare mixture of high-energy enlisted men and intelligent officers that made good regiments, but this was a façade.

The Fifty-third was not what it appeared to be. The regiment was not composed of what was referred to as "good stock," but with whatever men D'Epineuil could drag into his ranks. Only 130 Frenchmen, mostly officers and sergeants, had served in the regiment, and few had any prior service in any army. The rest of the regiment's makeup was a varied as the country itself, including a company of Tuscarora Indians from rural New York State. Many of the men were dirty and unkempt, having not been instructed on how to keep themselves clean by their uneducated officers. Because of this, disease was rampant in their camp. The uniform they wore was an imagination out of whole cloth as well. There was no Sixth Regiment of Imperial Guard Zouaves. D'Epineuil had just announced that to draw in more recruits. But the biggest charade was D'Epineuil himself. Before the war, he had been known for many things; he was a huckster or charlatan, involved in mostly illegal or at least inappropriate pursuits, but never a military officer. The regiment's only bright spot was the lieutenant colonel, Joseph Vigneur de Monteil. Unlike D'Epineuil, de Monteil, ten years older than his obnoxious colonel, was well regarded in the French community in New York City and a military veteran. Taken in by patriotic fervor for his adopted nation, de Monteil joined D'Epineuil and overlooked his obvious military shortcomings, unwittingly giving the Zouaves validity in New York City's societal circles. There was trouble brewing in the regiment, and it bubbled just below the surface.[30]

Burnside's next regiment was having growing pains as well. The Twenty-first Massachusetts, which had been stationed in the area since September guarding the rail line to Annapolis, was witnessing a power play at the top. Colonel Augustus Morse—who, as one regimental writer described him, "though of a kindly disposition, he was of a lazy habit, entirely destitute of soldiery enthusiasm or spirit, wonderfully ignorant of military drill and maneuvers, and a wretched disciplinarian"—was a poor officer. Few could pardon him for leaving the regiment in the hot Maryland sun for an hour while he paid his respects to the Baltimore commander that August. Nor would they understand why they had been selected to load the supplies for Sherman's Port Royal Expedition only to watch it sail away without them. The regiment needed a more energetic commander.[31]

It received just such a man in Lieutenant Colonel Alberto C. Maggi, a no-nonsense disciplinarian who had served with Garibaldi in Italy before immigrating to Massachusetts. The fiery Italian took an immediately dislike to the easygoing New England officer, and soon Maggi was placed under arrest. But the Twenty-first's rank and file saw that Maggi was the kind of officer they wanted to take them into battle, so they began a letter-writing campaign to Governor John Andrew, Massachusetts senators and even the secretary of war to weigh in on the argument in the regiment's favor. All agreed that Morse was not the man for the position, but would the decision makers see it that way? The men would just have to wait.[32]

Nearly a month would pass before the next members of the expedition marched into Annapolis. Meanwhile, supplies were gathered and soldiers were drilled. The next regiment arrived late on the night of December 13 at the Annapolis docks. It was commanded by the youngest colonel in Burnside's little army, Thomas G. Stevenson, a boyish twenty-five-year-old. Stevenson's regiment had at its core one of the best-drilled militia companies in New England, known as the "New England Guard." A former cashier for a railroad, Stevenson and his militiamen filled twenty-eight officer positions out of thirty-eight in the regiment. With such experience, the Twenty-fourth Massachusetts was quickly catching up to drill with some of the older veteran regiments.[33]

Five days after the Twenty-fourth's arrival, Connecticut's third contribution, the Eleventh Connecticut arrived under Colonel T.H.C. Kingsbury, and two weeks later, one of the few regiments recruited with Burnside's Expedition in mind arrived. The Fifth Rhode Island Battalion was recruited solely for coastal service and even advertised no fatiguing marches for its members. The battalion would be deployed to aid the naval forces, supplementing their cannon crews, as well as occupy fortifications and more sedentary positions. At least, that was the intention.[34]

Burnside had foreseen a campaign without the use of regular light artillery batteries, as the troops would not be too far without naval support. He had imagined small, lightweight howitzers dragged by their service crews, one or two horses or pulled by the infantry regiments themselves as needed, but Burnside was practical as well, and he knew that a light artillery battery might give him the range and punch that the lightweight howitzers could not. He also planned on the artillerymen to supervise any siege warfare that the expedition might encounter, so as his troops began to coalesce around Annapolis, Burnside requested a light artillery battery to accompany his excursion. The War Department approved the request and sent Battery F, First Rhode Island, under Captain James Belger, which arrived on December 20 to join Burnside's little army. Belger, a ten-year artillery veteran, was a better choice than Burnside could have expected, and Belger's four ten-pounder Parrott rifle cannons and two twelve-pounder howitzers were the perfect combination for both long- and short-range operations.[35]

Now that Burnside's little army was taking shape, he needed senior officers to command it. He chose three men whom he had befriended during his time at West Point. Unlike Burnside, all three had stayed in the army and made their careers there. These were just the kind of men to support the general while he rushed about gathering the necessary items for the expedition.

Their friendship created a built-in rapport that other commanders could only hope for with a trust that was inherent.

The first brigade commander and Burnside's second in command arrived in late October and immediately took over the troops assembling outside Annapolis. Burnside left the new arrival, Brigadier General John Gray Foster, to see about supplies and transportation, leaving Foster in charge. John Foster was already a kind of Union hero. Having graduated in the class prior to Burnside's, Foster, a New Hampshire native, had served in the vaunted engineer corps, seeing service in Mexico. His bravery in the campaign that took Mexico City promoted him temporarily to the rank of captain, but it also wounded him severely. After the war, Foster's duties as an engineer placed him in various positions, including as a member of the Coast Survey office and a stint as a teacher at West Point. He spent the years leading up to the war overseeing fort construction on the East Coast, and it was in this capacity that he found himself in Fort Sumter during the Secession Crisis and its bombardment. Serving under Major Robert Anderson, Foster had commanded a section of the fort's cannons in that valiant but doomed

defense. A tall and stoic commander, Foster was never photographed out of uniform. Every button buttoned and his military posture showed the professional that he was. Many of the volunteers under him saw Foster as a strict but fair disciplinarian, a commander who knew his occupation.[36]

John G. Foster had served at Fort Sumter in 1861 and was Burnside's second in command. *From the Library of Congress.*

December brought the other two brigade commanders to the army. Jesse L. Reno's career paralleled that of Foster's. Born in Pennsylvania in 1823, Reno graduated in the same class as Foster and began his army career as an ordnance officer in New York until the Mexican War called. There, Reno commanded a howitzer battery and, like Foster, was promoted and wounded. After the war, Reno also served as an instructor at West Point and then was on a board that rewrote the drill manual for large artillery cannons. In the immediate years before secession, Reno had been stationed at the Mount Vernon Arsenal in Alabama. In 1861, Reno was captured by Alabama

A fierce and energetic fighter, Jesse Reno would lead from the front. This caused him to be killed, accidentally, by his own men on South Mountain, September 14, 1862. *From the Library of Congress.*

state forces, and the arsenal was seized. Paroled and sent northward soon after, Reno was promoted to brigadier general in November and happily joined Burnside's little army soon thereafter. Stocky, well-built Reno sported a black full beard and mustache as well as twin widow peaks advancing up from his temples. Where Foster was careful and focused, Reno was energetic. One of the Pennsylvanians described him best: "On the field of action, the whole man loomed up as inspiration, a magnet, yes a dynamo to his men. Enthusiasm was one of his native characteristics." Where others said, "Go there," Reno's mantra was "Follow me."[37]

With a piercing gaze and muttonchops comparable to his commanding officer's, the third brigade commander John Grubb Parke was combination of Foster's intelligence and Reno's energy. Born in Pennsylvania, Parke graduated from the Point two years after Burnside and was the youngest of the generals. Like the commander, Parke's military career was peacetime service. As a topographical engineer, Parke settled boundaries and served as a secretary of the internal improvement boards. Unlike the other two, Parke

An expert engineer and organizer, Parke would eventually command the Ninth Corps. *From the Library of Congress.*

had formally been raised to the rank of captain for his services in 1861, while Reno and Foster's promotions had been only field temporary. Parke's lack of combat service was his only detriment, one that would hopefully be remedied quickly.[38]

With the commanders present, Burnside ordered the regiments into three brigades. Foster's command consisted of the Twenty-third, Twenty-fourth, Twenty-fifth and Twenty-seventh Massachusetts and the Tenth Connecticut Regiments. The remainder, which had been in a temporary brigade under Colonel Harland of the Eighth Connecticut, was divided between Reno and Parke. Reno's troops were numbered as the Second Brigade with the two Fifty-firsts and the Twenty-first Massachusetts, while Parke's Third Brigade paired up the two Connecticut regiments, the Eighth and Eleventh, with Fifth Rhode Island Battalion and the unkempt Fifty-third New York. More troops were needed to complete the army, and they soon began to arrive.[39]

By January, Burnside still needed some regiments to fill his fifteen-thousand-man quota as detailed in McClellan's orders. Finding his usual sources dried up, Burnside appealed directly to his old friend. No longer encumbered by perceived political favoritism, McClellan offered to make up the difference from the main army. As an added bonus, he allowed Burnside to review the troops stationed around D.C. and to choose the ones that he thought suited the operation best.

The first regiment that Burnside chose had a strange history with the general already. The Fourth Rhode Island Infantry had been recruited in Providence and was retained by Governor William Sprague as a show regiment. Burnside had reviewed it in September and was very impressed, but the governor flatly refused a request for the regiment to join the expedition. Sprague said the regiment was not trained for amphibious operations and would be ruined if it was so used. Burnside would have to get another regiment; the Fourth was not for him. So it was until January 1862. Until then, the Fourth Rhode Island had been sent to join the main army in October and had marched across the District of Columbia and north-central Maryland from one muddy camp to another and from one brigade to another. Its colonel had run afoul of the politically savvy Governor Sprague and was dismissed, being replaced by a hard-faced First Rhode Island captain with piercing blue eyes and a rather odd middle name for a soldier, Isaac Peace Rodman. Rodman had served under Burnside at Manassas, and with McClellan's blessing, the Fourth Rhode Island was transferred to Burnside's command. Rodman, unpopular at first, soon won over his regiment, and as they left for the trains to Annapolis, Rodman sported a new set of field glasses paid for by the regiment.[40]

The next regiment that Burnside applied for was the Ninth New Jersey Infantry. Recruited from central New Jersey, the regiment was oversized, having two extra companies. However, under the careful hand of Lieutenant Colonel Charles A. Heckman, it performed capably. Heckman's superior, Joseph Allen, a civil engineer by trade with no military experience, at least had the good sense of not meddling where he was out of his league. Burnside was impressed, and soon orders were cut for the Ninth New Jersey to join the expedition.[41]

The last regiment to join the expedition did so by the skin of its teeth. The Eighty-ninth New York, nicknamed the "Dickinson Guard" after a local politician in Elmira, had just arrived in the area and was still sorting itself out when orders came for it to join the expedition. One day, it received its new rifles, and the next day, it was heading for Annapolis. When it arrived at Annapolis, it was thrown immediately aboard a troop transport without any rations except hardtack and water. It was enough to make heads spin.[42]

The new arrivals were split between the Second and Third Brigades with the Ninth New Jersey joined to Reno's command and the Fourth Rhode Island and Eighty-ninth New York attached to Parke's brigade. Few of the regiments fit Burnside's original plan for seafarers to act in accordance with the navy, but it had been gotten up with such alacrity that Burnside was lucky to get what he did get. As the troops marched the two miles from the camps into Annapolis and the waiting transports, they struck up a marching tune popular then known as "Marching Along." One verse started with the line, "The army is gathering from near and from far, the trumpet is sounding the call for the war." But with the next line, the men, showing their newfound faith in Burnside, substituted his name in the place of McClellan's, so that they sang:

> Burnside's our leader he's gallant and strong,
> so gird on the armor and go marching along.

His fifteen thousand men, three generals and one light artillery battery made a formidable army, and it was up to him to use it. Burnside had the army but wondered about the navy.

# "A Strange Incongruous Medley"

With his army coming together in the late fall at Annapolis, Burnside needed a navy to transport and protect them. If he had thought recruiting regiments was difficult, ship recruitment would be worse. Expeditions like Burnside's were forced to compete for the limited resources available for an amphibious operation. At the same time Sherman's expedition to Port Royal was taking shape and sapping Burnside's resources, General Benjamin Butler was mounting an expedition of his own, launching from Hampton Roads, Virginia. Everywhere ships were in short supply, and as per McClellan's orders, Burnside had to supplement his fleet with gunboats, adding to Burnside's distress. If Burnside's Coastal Division was to fulfill its initial obligation, that of being seaborne, Burnside would need a wily naval officer to aid him. And that is just what Burnside had. Commander Samuel F. Hazard, a fifty-seven-year-old Rhode Islander, had been in the navy for thirty-eight years, both behind the desk and on the water. He had seen action at every naval posting except the East Indian Ocean, but when the war broke out, Hazard was sidelined to give more active officers sea commands. The old commander had spent most of the summer organizing western gunboat fleets, until he had been ordered to command Fort Wool on the Rip Raps, a crumbling fort located just off shore from Fort Monroe in Hampton Roads. The seafarer could see the writing on the wall that it was time to retire, but the patriotic Rhode Islander felt he had more to give, and when Burnside asked for a naval aide for his command, Hazard leapt at the chance.[43]

The Naval Academy at Annapolis, Maryland, in 1853. The academy's grounds were used as the loading point for Burnside's Expedition. *From* New York Illustrated Newspaper, *1853*.

While Burnside canvassed the North for regiments, Hazard searched the northern ports for available ships. This hodgepodge fleet would act independently of the U.S. Navy and be under Hazard's and Burnside's orders. The ships had to be shallow on the draft to work the inland rivers but durable enough to last the trip through ocean seas to arrive at their destination. There had to be a mix of sail and steam to give versatility to Burnside's operations, but the ships had to be able to carry large loads of men and material. Burnside also tasked Hazard with arming several of the ships with cannons to protect the infantry without relying on the navy ships too much, as per McClellan's directive. These ships ran the gambit from tugboats to sailing vessels, with a few canalboats to be used as floating batteries.[44]

Hazard's impromptu fleet began arriving at Annapolis in December and came in every shape and size. There was the sailing schooner *Highlander*, which was originally the 561-ton pine wood carrier *Claremont* from New Jersey. Employed as an armed transport, its hold was soon outfitted with three-level bunks that barely fit in the ship's hold, leaving little maneuvering room for the two hundred men who were assigned to it. With only thirty inches between the bunk rows, the Twenty-third Massachusetts soldiers assigned to the ship felt like sardines. Also crammed below with the Bay Staters was Elias Smith of the *New York Times*, one of over a dozen war correspondents coming to record Burnside's campaign.

Beside *Highland*er stood the steamer *Hussar*, reconfigured to carry the rest of the Twenty-third Massachusetts. Armed with a two pairs of thirty-pounder Parrott rifled cannons and the more mobile six-pound Wiard steel guns, the *Hussar* was a larger antebellum hay freighter. Bulky and painted black, the men soon nicknamed it the "blacksmith shop."[45]

The bulk of the Twenty-fifth Massachusetts crammed on the steamer *New York*, while Companies D and H squeezed onto the steam propeller gunboat *Zouave*. The Tenth Connecticut, like the Twenty-fifth Massachusetts, was divided between a large steamer, *New Brunswick*, and a schooner, *E.W. Farrington*. Those Connecticut troops aboard the *New Brunswick* also had Brigadier General Foster and staff enfolded with them.[46]

The bark *Guerilla* was originally the slave ship *Mary Jane Kimball*, which had been caught trying to run a load of African slaves through the newly initiated Union blockade. The "cargo" was returned to Africa, and the captain was executed as per United States law; the ship was confiscated and pressed into military service. Its hold was cleaned up and the chains were removed, but the racks that held slaves were left in place to accommodate its new military cargo: the Twenty-seventh Massachusetts. Those who could not fit on the *Kimball* were transferred to the gunboat *Ranger*.[47]

Jesse Reno's brigade was similarly shipped out. Reno and staff joined the Twenty-first Massachusetts aboard the steamer *Northerner*. The Twenty-first Massachusetts was missing one crucial member as it filed aboard. The regiment's letter-writing campaign had succeeded, and Colonel Morse was ordered to remain as commander of the soon-to-be-empty Annapolis post. Before the fleet sailed, Morse, who received a cold reception from his former regiment, bade them farewell, inappropriately saying to the men when they were in a battle to stay in action until they "lost some men." The joke fell flat, and with that, the Twenty-first Massachusetts passed into the hands of the Italian lieutenant colonel.[48]

The Fifty-first New York was split and sardined onto two small propeller gunboats, the *Lancer* and *Pioneer*. The Ninth New Jersey and Fifty-first Pennsylvania were each given a steamer and a sailing vessel for their troops. The steamer *Cossack*, which carried the majority of the Fifty-first Pennsylvania, also carried the majority of the newspapermen who were accompanying the expedition. The Sixth New Hampshire, a late arrival, was put aboard the side-wheeler steamer *Louisiana* and schooner *Maria Greenwood*, still loaded with coal and other supplies and lashed to the *Louisiana*'s side. The Granite State men just would have to make do.[49]

In Parke's brigade, the Eighth Connecticut crammed aboard the bark *H.D. Brookman* and the gunboat *Chasseur*, while the Eleventh Connecticut was packed into the bark *Voltigeur* and gunboat *Sentinel*. Like the others, the Fifth Rhode Island was divided between two ships, but half of the undersized regiment stretched out on the *Kitty Simpson*, while the other half was forced to make room for the Twenty-fifth Massachusetts's Company I aboard the schooner *Skirmisher*. Belger's Battery was split with the men and horses put aboard the steamer *George Peabody*, while the equipment was placed on the schooner *John T. Brady*.[50]

While some regiments were crammed aboard little ships with limited space, others had rather pleasant accommodations. The Fourth Rhode Island and the Eighty-ninth drew the best accommodations. The Fourth Rhode Island's *Eastern Queen*, a chartered steamship passenger liner that plied the Boston to Portland, Maine route, was easily equipped to carry the Rhode Islanders and their equipment with room to spare. The Eighty-ninth was placed on the last-minute arrival *Aracan*, which was a palatial passenger line from Boston, chartered to replace another vessel that had blown its boiler making for Annapolis. Other ships had shadier pasts.[51]

Not all of the ships had been procured with patriotism in mind. The bark *John Trucks* was a hard-luck ship. In February 1861, the *Trucks* had been staved in by an ice floe while unloading its cargo at a Philadelphia wharf. The ship then slid on the muddy bottom of the Delaware River and into the shipping lanes. In June, the wreck was involved in at least two separate collisions, causing serious damage to passing vessels. Forced to alleviate the problem, a salvage team dragged the ship back to the wharf and began to pump it out. In doing so, they found the bodies of two men who had been missing since the ship sank. A hard-luck ship deserves a hard-luck regiment, and the fractious Zouaves under Colonel D'Epineuil drew the newly raised *John Trucks*. Crammed aboard the ship were the 750 men and D'Epineuil's wife, incognito.[52]

Burnside's auxiliary forces were also disposed aboard ships for transit. Intending to be a self-sufficient military entity, Burnside's fleet would be carrying a battery of siege mortars and a French-style pontoon bridge of India rubber that could cover a span over five thousand feet. A submarine explosives expert and assistants with over one hundred pounds of gunpowder, mines and batteries to detonate the explosives were crammed into the schooner *Edward Slade* in case any demolition was necessary. Five old canalboats, to be used as floating batteries, were added to the fleet, being towed southward. One final addition was a contingent of seventy-five men from the Signal Corps who crowded on the *Colonel Slattery* just as the first boats were pushing from the Annapolis wharf.[53]

By January 9, the assembled fleet of nine steam-powered gunboats, eight small and four large steamers, two hospital ships, twenty-four sailing vessels of various sizes, six towed boats and various supply vessels was heading southward. The fleet, led by Burnside in the gunboat *Picket*, was so large that it was still leaving the next day. After almost six months of nearly constant hectic military movements, the colonial town returned to its quiet, peaceful existence along the Severn River.[54]

The trip southward should have been uneventful, but the best plans turn on the whim of the littlest things. As Burnside's fleet passed the Potomac River's mouth, sixty miles southward, the fleet ran into a heavy fog bank, turning the night an inky black. In their quickness to get the ships and men moving, no one had planned for this contingency. The only orders the ships' captains received were to "follow the lead vessel." The ships were supposed to make their way in their own time to Hampton Roads. Some ships, like Reno's *Northerner*, made the journey with little complications, but farther up the bay, the rest of the fleet was floundering. The Twenty-fifth Massachusetts in the *New York* reported that at midday it could not see more than half a ship's length, so thick was the fog. With such dense conditions it is no wonder that some accidents occurred. The gunboat *Sentinel* was towing the *Voltigeur* and the hard-luck *John Trucks* when they became wrapped in the fog blanket. The *Trucks*, drawing more water than the others, suddenly hit a sandbar and stuck fast. The *Sentinel's* tow cable snapped, and it disappeared into the fog, but the *Trucks* wasn't out of danger yet. The *Voltigeur*, towed behind the *Trucks*, soon overtook the grounded vessel and crashed into it. The *Voltigeur* then broke its tow cable, and it, too, passed into the fog bank, leaving the Zouaves stuck alone on the sandbar. The *Martha Greenwood* broadsided a schooner, but fortunately, both ships were traveling slow enough that damage was minimal. All through the night and into the next morning, boat whistles and drum taps sounded in the fog banks to announce the presence of the bound ships, but the fog finally burned off by the afternoon. The fleet, except for those noticeable accidents, soon made up the delay and reached Fort Monroe off the tip of the Virginia Peninsula.[55]

With so many different kinds of ships, it took some time for them all to assemble at the fort. While the fleet gathered in the shadow of Fort Monroe, some major changes occurred. The *Martha Greenwood*, although only lightly

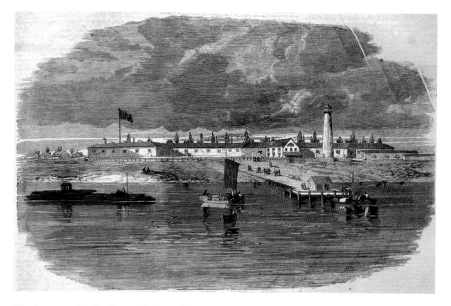

The first stop for the Burnside Expedition was Fort Monroe at the southern end of the Chesapeake Bay. *From* London Illustrated News, *May 20, 1861.*

damaged, took advantage of the delay to relieve itself of the soldiers of the Sixth New Hampshire. The men were crowded into the *Louisiana* with the rest of the regiment. The *Martha Greenwood* soon made repairs, but the soldiers never transferred back, causing a certain amount of complaining.[56]

Just before the fleet ventured on, an additional soldier joined them at Fort Monroe. Joseph de Monteil, formerly of the Fifty-third New York, approached Burnside to join the expedition. He offered to serve in any capacity, even as a private soldier. What would have made the lieutenant colonel so desperate? It had quickly become evident at the Annapolis camp that the Fifty-third New York was commanded by an unstable person. D'Epineuil, paranoid to distraction, felt that de Monteil, who had served in the French army, was becoming too popular with the men. Under de Monteil, the men were learning their trade, but D'Epineuil and a cadre of incompetent officers jealously conspired to break the lieutenant colonel and drive him from the unit before their incompetency was revealed. D'Epineuil therefore preferred charges against de Monteil. In the final weeks of December, D'Epineuil had de Monteil court-martialed before a court of junior regimental officers for drunkenness, neglect of duty and disrespectful language. Not surprisingly, de Monteil was found guilty; he requested another court-martial, this time before officers from outside the regiment. This inquiry found de Monteil innocent and reinstated him, but the shamed D'Epineuil continued to persecute his lieutenant colonel. The men, who had a reputation for sloppiness and riot, soon mutinied, claiming the officers were abusing them. Embarrassed, D'Epineuil resulted to draconian measures and clamped down on his men, while an assassination attempt soon drove de Monetil from the camp. Making his way to General McClellan's headquarters while Burnside was loading his expedition, de Monetil sought aid. McClellan suggested de Monetil looked guilty deserting his post, but if he sought Burnside out and tendered his services, all would be forgiven. Burnside was moved by the story and readily accepted to elder Frenchman back to the expedition, and as the Fifty-third, aboard the *John Trucks*, was still stuck fast near the Potomac River and would miss the expedition's next advance, the point was moot.[57]

Assembling ahead of Burnside's fleet at sea was Flag Officer Louis M. Goldsborough's covering fleet. Goldsborough looked rumpled and doughy and dressed like a tugboat captain with a simple pilot's cap and an undress naval frock coat. He stood a resounding six foot, four inches tall and weighed a tremendous three hundred pounds. On his roundish face, he sported a thick red beard. His men had given him the nickname "Old Guts," and he was generally well liked. Like Hazard, he had been a courageous junior officer and seen action during the Mexican War, but since then, Goldsborough had served in a chain of less-active

Flag Officer Louis M. "Old Guts" Goldsborough led the naval portion of Burnside's Expedition. *From U.S. Naval Historical Center, Washington, D.C.*

duty stations, including as superintendent of the Naval Academy in the 1850s and commander of the Brazilian Squadron. He had been made commander of the recently divided Atlantic Blockading Squadron, retaining command of the northern section from its former commander, Flag Officer Silas Stringham, in September 1861. He joined Burnside's expedition, to personally take command of his gathering fleet, aboard the transport *S.R. Spaulding*.[58]

Hazard and Burnside had gathered nearly seventy ships as they readied to put to sea. George Hollis, one of Goldsborough's lieutenants, was not surprised by the amorphous nature of Burnside's fleet but merely disgusted. "What shall I call them? Not ships, but *craft*, which was the peculiar character of aspiration of forces upon the Chief of the Navy Department," commented the young sailor. His keen nautical mind accurately described them as "tug boats of all ages and fashions, side wheel and screw; little coasting and river steamers hardly fit to voyage from Boston to Cape Cod." Hollis remembered the fleet as "a strange incongruous medley."[59]

Everything was finally ready by January 11. Burnside's little fleet made its way to the ocean, and after the ships had rounded Cape Henry around 9:00 p.m., the captains all opened their sealed orders. They scanned the orders for a destination, and their eyes were immediately drawn to one line: "When off Cape Hatteras, throw overboard ballast, and run into the inlet." They finally knew their destination: Cape Hatteras. Soldiers cheered and sailors prayed. After four months of training and waiting, the troops would at last get to show their bravery. For the sailors, the waters of Cape Hatteras have a different name: the "Graveyard of the Atlantic." Tears would be shed and cheers would be cried before it was over. As the fleet passed into the Atlantic Ocean, a freshening breeze greeted the seasick soldiers, and a clear night sky cheered them, but for many of the seasoned seafarers, the weather was an omen that a different kind a storm was brewing.[60]

4

# "It Strikes Me that We Should Command the Waters of the Pamlico Sound"

O f course, Burnside and his higher officers knew where they were going long before the recent packets of orders were opened. The destination was Hatteras Inlet, as part of an overarching plan.

North Carolina was a state of strange dichotomies. It had a great coasting and seafaring tradition and a 350-mile coastline, but while its men were known for sailing the seas, its home-built ships were mostly inland sailers, and the coast was only broken by five navigable harbors. From the Virginia border, the barrier islands that made up the Outer Banks limited access to three of these harbors—the ones at the Ocracoke, Hatteras and Oregon Inlets. Farther south, two actual ports, Beaufort and Wilmington, provided the only direct sea routes for the state's exports.[61]

The Tarheel State had not quickly joined the fledgling Confederacy. It was, in fact, the last state to join the rebellion. Slavery, one of the cornerstones of the new nation-state, was not the powerbase here as it was in the Deep South. Few plantations with large slaveholdings existed in North Carolina, almost exclusively along its interior coast and middle or Piedmont areas, and in the western part of the state, slavery was all but unheard of among the hardscrabble farmers. Ironically, the largest single slave owners in the state, the Quakers of the Piedmont, had been quietly circumventing the law by treating the enslaved as freemen renters or transferring them to their brethren in northern states for eventual freedom.[62]

Before the advent of U.S. income tax, the poorest of the poor were located on the fringes, east and west, of the state and saw very little in return for their taxes, causing no little sense of consternation. North Carolina had been a close trading partner with Virginia, and rail and canal creation reflected this. Rail lines and roads that brought the agricultural products to market were almost all created in the middle of the state, toward Petersburg, Norfolk and Richmond. The only north–south connecting rail line ran through eastern North Carolina. Once the state joined the rebellion, trains ran daily on the Weldon Railroad carrying men and war material to Richmond and Norfolk. The problem was that this valuable rail line ranged only 80 to 150 miles from the North Carolina coastline.[63]

Canals—a quick transportation system utilizing North Carolina's waterlogged eastern rivers and swamps—provided another way to transit goods to the north. The Dismal Swamp Canal and Chesapeake and Albemarle Canal systems grew out of the War of 1812, when the Chesapeake Bay had been blockaded by the British; now the canals were funneling crucial supplies and information to Norfolk and its environs.[64]

Few if any economic improvements were visited upon the poor parts of the state. What brought the state to join the rebellion was President Lincoln's call for seventy-five thousand militia volunteers to put down the Confederacy. Familial ties being stronger than nationalism, the state joined the Confederacy and would eventually send more troops to the Confederacy's armies than any other state except Virginia.[65]

In May 1861, when the state joined its sister states of the South in armed rebellion, volunteers rallied to the state's colors in the thousands, but weapons and uniforms were in short supply. Militia companies were quickly bounded together into regiments and sent to protect Richmond and Virginia from the Yankee hordes, leaving behind those who had to make do with whatever equipment was available. Unlike other states, North Carolina would set up an effective uniform and armaments system, but in January 1862, it was only in its infancy. Until the war manufacturing systems could catch up, the Confederacy would have to import its needs from friendly European powers. In this, North Carolina was geographically well placed. Located nearer to the British contraband ports in the Bahamas and Bermuda than any other Southern port—with the exception of blockaded Savannah, Georgia, and Charleston, South Carolina—North Carolina's ports were vitally important to the arming of the nation-state's soldiers.[66]

The state's ports, transportation systems, rail connections, food production and manpower pool should have made the state's defense a priority but instead became a contentious issue. Several times throughout the war, North

Carolina asked Virginia for aid in defending its territory, either by releasing North Carolina soldiers or supplies, but to no avail. President Jefferson Davis's Confederate War Department, more worried about massing Union forces in front of the Confederacy, was convinced that the battle was in the Chesapeake Bay basin, and few supplies were ever sent southward. Therefore, troops available to stop the Union forces had limited resources.[67]

Already, North Carolina's defenses had been tested and found lacking. In August 1861, General Benjamin Butler brought a small naval force backed up by two regiments and a battery of light artillery to take on Hatteras Inlet. The naval force pounded the forts at the inlet for two days and captured the harbor with little effort. In the ensuing panic, the Confederate forces abandoned the organic defenses that had been built at the other two inlets, surrendering three of North Carolina's five ports without a real fight.[68]

State officials and local Confederate commanders finally saw the danger they were in. With the state's defenses still unfinished, troops were hurried to the coast to limit the penetration of Union attacks. The only problem was that the Union forces were content to remain at Hatteras. A small skirmish over a Union outpost at Chicamacomico on the Outer Banks convinced both sides to sit behind their earthworks and await further developments. So as the Union crouched under the guns of several gunboats at Hatteras Inlet, the Confederates retired to Roanoke Island.[69]

In November 1861, Union military interests turned toward Roanoke Island. Newly appointed flag officer of the North Atlantic Blockading Squadron, Louis Goldsborough, frustrated by the lack of action in the reduction and occupation of Norfolk, wrote to Secretary of the Navy Gideon Wells with a proposition:

> It strikes me that we should command the waters of the Pamlico Sound, and this may, I think be easily accomplished if I can be given a few suitable vessels in addition to those already at Hatteras Inlet. The enemy now have seven or eight small but well-armed steamers on those waters, and these I propose to attack and subdue…This done, something further may be attempted in the way of driving the enemy away from Roanoke Island by a combined attack on the part of the Army and the Navy, ascending Albemarle Sound, destroying the lock or locks thereabouts of the canal between it and Norfolk and this effectively cutting off all inland communications.[70]

Goldsborough, who had been the first commanding officer of the Depot of Charts and Instruments in the 1830s, knew what he was suggesting: a combined army task force to storm the North Carolina sounds. At the same

Hawkins and his Zouaves. *From the Library of Congress.*

time Goldsborough was presenting his plan to his chief, a dapper young colonel was in Washington, D.C., to present the same idea to his chief.[71]

Rush Christopher Hawkins was a tall and handsome New York City lawyer, sporting a manicured goatee and athletic build. Prior to the war, Hawkins had married into the Brown family of Providence, Rhode Island, for which the Ivy League university had been named. Well educated and exceeding wealthy, Hawkins recruited his regiment of Zouaves in less than a week and outfitted their Arabic-inspired clothing himself. The regiment already had a reputation for a fine appearance on the parade ground but a fractious one among its officers. Hawkins lived by a credo that ruffled more than a few feathers. "I believe in unconditional honesty," he wrote, which caused more than one conflict in his military career.[72]

In fact, it was one such conflict that had brought him to Washington, D.C. In September, a captain from another regiment, Leon Barnard, had been forced out of his regiment for killing a soldier. Pulling some political strings, Barnard had himself transferred to Hawkins's Ninth New York Volunteer

48

Infantry, which was at that point garrisoning at Hatteras Inlet. Barnard's appointment rankled men and officers, and Hawkins complained about the outsider imposed on his military family. The complaint drew the ire of his superiors, and Hawkins was ordered to stand before a court-martial for insubordination. Ever the lawyer, Hawkins took the court-martial right to the top of the military command structure and demanded a personal meeting with President Lincoln.[73]

Hawkins's objectives in meeting Lincoln were twofold. He already had been exonerated by his superiors at Hampton Roads, but he wanted to take the moral high ground with the president and have Barnard removed from his regiment. Hawkins had no way of knowing, but his men had accomplished the task while he was away. The enlisted men in Barnard's company threatened him by night and refused to obey him during the day. Fellow officers refused to help him, and when a threat was scrawled on his tent one night, Barnard took the hint and resigned. Hawkins's other reason for meeting with the president was to lay before Lincoln his plan to retake North Carolina, using his little base at Hatteras Inlet as the staging area.[74]

Hawkins had been with Butler during the August assault on the inlet. Soon after the battle smoke cleared, Butler left to report the news to Lincoln personally, leaving Hawkins in command of the inlet for a month and a half. While in command, Hawkins had nearly 250 "Bankers" or locals seek his protection and sign an oath of allegiance to the Union. Many told the Union colonel that they never really wanted to secede and that many more in the interior of the state would flock to the flag if the Union just made an effort. Hawkins, overly confident, estimated that as much as a third of the state would rejoin the Union if the effort was made.

His plan was simple: using Hatteras to gather the naval and military forces, they would take Roanoke Island and its garrison, allowing further occupation of coastal North Carolina. Extra light draft ships sent by the navy would command the state's inland waterways, and Beaufort on the coast would be captured. Extra arms would be given to loyalists to protect their homes and project Union military power farther inland. An ebullient Hawkins wrote that "seven thousand men judiciously placed on the soil of North Carolina, would, within three weeks, draw twenty thousand Confederate troops from Virginia."[75]

Hawkins's superior, General John Wool, had approved the idea, and now it was before Lincoln. The president was visibly impressed with the hope of reclaiming one-third of one of the strongest Confederate states and sent Hawkins over to McClellan later that day, where he repeated his presentation to similar reception. Hawkins was ordered back to his regiment, confident that the plan had been accepted. There was no more talk of Leon Barnard, and he soon became a faint memory.[76]

McClellan had dispensed with the Coastal Division, operating with the main Army of the Potomac in November 1861, based on several key pieces of information. In an attempt to ease its supply issues, the main Confederate army had willingly relinquished its hold on the Potomac River's southern bank and the battlefield at Manassas. Instead, the army marched southward fifty miles to Fredericksburg, where it could more readily resupply its troops on stouter rails than the overworked Orange and Alexandria. This redeployment severely restricted Burnside's possible field of operations in the Chesapeake Bay. With the Confederate redeployment to Fredericksburg, Burnside's area of operations was halved. Because of this, Burnside's men would now be overmatched if they attempted to launch attacks on the Virginian shoreline. Coincidently, McClellan himself was putting the finishing touches on a large amphibious plan that would move most of his army to the Fort Monroe area and allow them to march on the Confederate capital, Richmond, before the Confederate army could react. With these two critical changes, the Chesapeake Bay became too small for Burnside's troops. This pushed Burnside farther south.[77]

With the navy asking for an expedition to the Outer Banks and the local commanders there telling of the potential for true success, McClellan sat down to plan out a suitable campaign. Although not knowing the area he was sending Burnside into, McClellan saw nothing but success and wrote the orders from his sickbed. In a long, rambling and somewhat overly detailed set of orders, McClellan combined elements of both Goldsborough's suggestion and Hawkins's report. He charged Burnside to first pass the treacherous Hatteras Inlet and assume command of the little garrison located there. He was then to, in combination with the navy, reduce or capture Roanoke Island and then strengthen the fortifications there, holding the island as his base of operations. Further actions by the navy would isolate the Confederate garrison at Norfolk.

After completing this first task, Burnside and Goldsborough would assault New Berne along the Neuse River, cutting off rail connections to the coast and the port of Beaufort. Once that was accomplished, the army was to march on Beaufort and its principal defense, Fort Macon, removing the port from Confederate hands. With these goals finished, Burnside was to destroy the vital north–south rail line that passed through Weldon at the railroad crossing at Goldsboro or some other point west. North Carolina's last port, Wilmington, was also an objective, and even the state capital, Raleigh, was not out of the question as a target. McClellan ended with some sage political advice for his protégé: McClellan suggested Burnside "should say as little as possible about politics or the negro."[78]

Three days before Burnside left Annapolis, the new Confederate commander arrived on Roanoke Island. He was a tall, gaunt man with graying hair, a wizened chin beard and piercing eyes that reminded some of an Old Testament prophet, but no description could be farther from the truth. Brigadier General Henry A. Wise was a hard-drinking, hard-cursing and hellfire secessionist. He was born in 1806 on Virginia's Delmarva Peninsula. Like many of Virginia's elite, he was privately tutored and became a lawyer, soon establishing a successful political career along the way. He was prolific and soon accrued a large family. His first wife died in a house fire, leaving him with four children. A second wife died in childbirth after adding at least five more children to the huge Wise clan. In 1853, Wise was married a third time and, by the end of his life, had sired fourteen children. Always politically connected, Wise bounced between the Virginia's Whig and Democratic Parties but always came out on top. In 1855, he became the state's thirty-third governor and presided over the John Brown Harper's Ferry crisis in 1859, signing Brown's death warrant as a last act in his position. Appointed to the state's secession convention in 1860, Wise was strident in his support of the Southern states that already had seceded. His eldest son, Obadiah, as editor of the *Richmond Enquirer*, acted as

An early photograph of Henry Wise. By late 1861, the dapper young man had morphed into a secessionist prophet. *From the Library of Congress.*

his father's mouthpiece, keeping up the steady drumbeat of secession. As the state drifted toward secession, it was Wise who had ordered the state's troops to take the Gasport Naval Yard at Norfolk, Virginia, saving the facilities for the Confederacy. But Wise's military career was not as bright as his political one.[79]

Rich and popular, Wise soon raised a legion, a mixed arms unit, with three regiments of infantry, two batteries of artillery and some companies of cavalry. Uniformed and armed through his money and prestige, the legion was one of the earliest organized larger units in the Confederate army. Recruited from across the state, the legion and Wise were first stationed in western Virginia, now West Virginia, to oppose Union thrusts from Ohio. Ever quick to voice his opinion, Wise soon ran afoul of his fellow officers and superiors. Constant bickering with the former thirty-first state governor and ex–secretary of war turned Confederate general John B. Floyd became a feud. Even their commander, Robert E. Lee, could not get the former governors to collaborate. The ensuing Kanawha Campaign was a series of disjointed and disorganized battles, with the Confederates driven from the area. In disgust, President Davis separated the generals, ordering Floyd to Tennessee and Wise to Roanoke Island. Davis made a clean slate of the fiasco by reassigning Lee as his personal military advisor, leaving the next general to clean up the department.[80]

What Wise saw on Roanoke Island was shocking. The "forts had no gunners, no rifled cannon, no supplies, no anything except undrilled and unpaid country bumpkins posing as troops," one writer recorded. With his legion still strung out on the march from western Virginia, Wise had to make do with the raw materials at hand. The two North Carolina regiments that garrisoned the island were in a dreadful condition, with "most of the men still carrying their own hunting rifles, shotguns and fowling pieces." Clothing barely covered the men's nakedness, and there was no sense of a uniform among the rank and file. What few supplies were landed on the island had been landed directly on the shoreline by rowboat, as there were no dock facilities. Beasts of burden to aid in moving the heavy guns and materials were two pairs of oxen and a few half-starved ponies. Musket ammunition was at such a premium that few of the soldiers had ever fired theirs on a target range or drill field. Artillery supplies were even more scarce with no rifled cannon shells for the forts' guns, and the field battery—consisting of a twenty-four-pounder howitzer, an eighteen-pounder Mexican War trophy and a small six-pounder light gun brought by one of the companies from its hometown—only had ammunition for the howitzer and the light gun.

No ammunition existed on the island for the trophy cannon. The island's defenses needed more of everything, from large-caliber cannons to the simplest nail. Wise had inherited a disaster in the making. But it had not always been like this.[81]

Beginning in August the year before, when Hatteras Inlet fell to Union forces, the Confederate realized the potential danger a Union attack could wreak. Colonel Ambrose Wright of the Third Georgia Infantry first recognized the island's defensive needs when a portion of his regiment was sent south to reinforce Hatteras Inlet. Turned back by the news of that installation's fall, Wright began entrenching on the island in September.[82]

Roanoke Island was only three miles wide and twelve miles long, but it was strategically placed in between two of North Carolina's large inland bodies of water, the Albemarle and Pamlico Sounds. The small island restricted access to any vessel venturing from one sound to the other. Union forces advancing from Hatteras would have to pass the island, and that is where the Confederates determined to make their stand. But otherwise, Roanoke Island was a queer choice. The island was decidedly swampy, with nearly half of it too swampy to drain off and farm. The locals were grouped in two small villages on the southern point and at a shallow harbor on the eastern shore. There were few roads, and most of the communication as well as the maritime occupations were done by ship. Those who did farm did so on small plots, barely eking out a living among the thick trees. Like many of those on the Outer Banks, they were apathetic to secession, with only a few votes against the Union in the secession conventions in May. Slaves were rare and mostly in smallholdings, farming, fishing or woodcutting, while the island did have a small freedmen population. Many of the locals just wanted to be left out of the war altogether.[83]

Under the professional eye of engineer Colonel Charles H. Dimmock, Wright began to lay out the fortifications on the western side of the island throughout the fall of 1861. With no naturally occurring rock, Dimmock planned on using sand and turf fortifications like those on the Outer Banks. He chose Pork Point, the nearest part of the island to the mainland, to construct his first entrenchment. Named after a Georgia colonel martyred at Manassas, Fort Bartow was built for eight guns to interdict the nearby shipping channel.[84]

To protect Fort Bartow's landward approaches, Wright needed a fort in the center of the island. South of the fort, a mile and a half along the main road, Wright had his men build a three-gun battery on an imperceptible rise in the swamp called Supple's Hill. When the Georgians, further reinforced

Charles Dimmock, designer of Roanoke Island's defenses, would go on to design even larger defenses, including those at Petersburg, Virginia. *From the National Park Service.*

by recently arrived impressed black laborers, marched down the road, they needed a local guide to point out the site, so undistinguished was its appearance. Supple's Hill was surrounded by the thick tar-like swamps that were the signature of the island. To the east, the swamp became more watery and was filled with sharp-bladed sawgrass, while on the west, the briars and tangle foot aided the defenders as if planted for that reason. The swamps on either side were of an unknown depth, slowing down any potential Union attack. To further protect it from Union artillery and give the defenders a surprise advantage, the battery was placed around the bend in the road. Beside the battery, entrenchments were constructed to give cover for supporting troops, while Wright had the trees cut down seven hundred yards from the battery to give it a larger field of fire. Given the limited resources the Confederates had, the battery was surprisingly strong.[85]

While the Georgians dug in the middle of the island, to the north, the newly arrived Eighth North Carolina Infantry was making the sand fly as well. Led by Rhode Island–born Henry M. Shaw, a forty-five-year-old local doctor, the Eighth was not enamored of its first duty post or its commander. Many of the men grumbled at the hard labor required of them as they built two more forts, Forts Blanchard and Huger. Evidently, Colonel Shaw did not take a vested interest in his duty, as one officer mentioned in his diary that Shaw mostly remained in his tent playing chess. Some felt Shaw was not worthy of the position but that powder and ball were too precious to kill him.

In the onerous duty of building forts, the Eighth was aided by the remnants of another North Carolina regiment, the Seventeenth. The

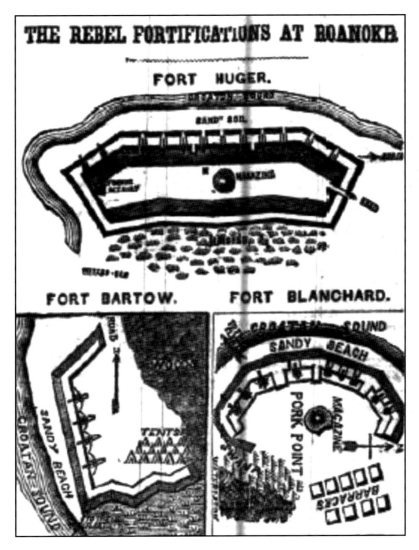

The only known maps concerning the main Confederate defenses were done by the *New York Herald* on February 24, 1862. While the illustrator correctly identified Fort Huger, he mixed up Forts Bartow and Blanchard. *From* New York Herald, *February 24, 1862.*

Seventeenth North Carolina Infantry had been stationed on the Outer Banks as soon as the state left the Union. It had garrisoned the sand forts that had covered the inlets at Ocracoke, Hatteras and Oregon. So when the Union assaulted Hatteras and captured the troops there, the vast majority were members of the Seventeenth. Only three companies, having evacuated

A Northerner by birth, Henry Marchmore Shaw was not a popular choice to lead the Eighth North Carolina. *From Walter Clark's* Histories of the Several Regiments and Battalions from North Carolina.

Ocracoke and Oregon Inlets, made it back to Roanoke Island, and only the heavy guns at Oregon were salvaged and added to the island's armament. Partially trained on the heavy guns, the three companies were soon assigned to artillery duty in newly constructed Fort Bartow under Major Gabriel Hill. As work began in earnest, a new general arrived to review the progress. As General Wise would later find out, the dreaded complacency that overtook the Confederates now would lead to ruin.[86]

Brigadier General Daniel Harvey Hill was a bonafide war hero for the fledgling Confederacy, having won the first land battle at Big Bethel, Virginia. A tall but stooping man, Hill had graduated from West Point in 1842. He taught mathematics and engineering at Washington College in Lexington, Virginia, where he met a fellow professor at a nearby military college. They were soon joined not just by profession but also by marriage, as they married sisters. Hill's brother-in-law would later be known as Stonewall Jackson. Hill later accepted a position at Davidson College in North Carolina and it was from there that he joined the army. After the Battle of Big Bethel, Hill was promoted and given the military Department of North Carolina, responsible for all military operations in eastern North Carolina, arriving in the area in late September.[87]

Hill immediately wrote down his concerns about his new command. Looking over the map, Hill correctly guessed Roanoke Island's importance to the Confederacy. Writing on October 18 to Secretary of the Confederate Navy Stephen Mallory, Hill stated, "Roanoke Island is the key of one third of North Carolina, and whose occupancy by the enemy would enable him to reach the great railroad from Richmond to New Orleans." Hill suggested that four additional regiments be sent to aid the garrison in defending the island and rifled cannons be installed in the new earthworks.[88]

After an inspection tour, Hill was even more adamant. He believed that the forts were strong but misplaced, while the three-gun battery at Supple's Hill was inadequate to stop a land attack. Hill, with a West Pointer's eye, felt that the earthwork should be supported by entrenchment across the entire width of the island, depending on manpower for defense and not on the whims of natural impediments like swamps to stem a Union tide. The work that had been begun with so much expediency when the Union troops were expected had cooled with the lack of action. "Our people are so lazy and inefficient that I am half inclined to quit in disgust," Hill wrote to his wife about the works on the island. There was also bad feeling between the

General D.H. Hill, a North Carolinian general and brother-in-law of "Stonewall" Jackson, eventually resigned in disgust at the Confederate lack of interest in defending, among other areas, Roanoke Island. *From the Library of Congress.*

North Carolina and Georgia regiments on the island. The Third Georgia was well disciplined, supplied and uniformed, while Shaw's Eighth North Carolina was not.[89]

Hill was also dismayed by the Confederate navy in North Carolina's waters. Although the Confederate government had just authorized boat purchases and construction to beef up the present fleet of seven steamer tugs and schooners, Hill felt it would not be enough. The fleet, which was dubbed the "Mosquito Fleet" by infantry comrades for its ability to only annoy the Union ships at their Hatteras base, was pitiful. Hill described it as "farcically unfit for wartime service." The fleet was under Commander William F. Lynch, a former U.S. Navy captain. Lynch's career had been one of exploration, including a mapping expedition to the Holy Land and the Dead Sea. Lynch's ships included five tugs, a side-wheeler steamer and the *Black Warrior*, a two-masted sailing schooner. The seven ships had between them only eight guns of various calibers. Since August 1861, they had done as well as possible to challenge the more suitably armed Union fleet at Hatteras, but for the most part, they merely demonstrated against the superior Union fleet. As the year ended, Lynch's fleet continued to annoy Union ships but did little fighting. Its one success had been just before Hill's inspection, when three of its ships had captured the Union screw tug *Fanny* off Chickamacomico on October 2. The prize was integrated into the fleet, replacing a ship that was lost the next month.[90]

Hill tried to rectify the situation. He hammered Richmond for more of everything, especially rifled cannons. Hill called on North Carolina's militia to rally on the island and buoy the defenders' numbers while demanding the state support the Eighth North Carolina's needs. On all these points he was rebuffed. Secretary Mallory, in charge of the heavy guns located at the Norfolk naval yard, just passed the request on to the garrison commander of Norfolk, Brigadier General Benjamin Huger. Huger, who was described as the "barnacle on the Confederacy," felt that at any time Union forces stationed across the Chesapeake Bay would attack his weakened city and refused to part with any of the pieces. Supplies for the North Carolina troops were delayed. An emergency call out of North Carolina's eastern militia by Hill netted only five hundred men, and many of them did not show. Hill complained to the governor. In response to his constituents, Governor Clark of North Carolina rebuked Hill for needlessly calling out the militia when there was no threat of danger. Hill, angered beyond words, immediately put in his request for a transfer posthaste. He would not serve in a state where he had to serve so many masters at one time. Reluctantly, he left his home state for service in the main army after less than two months in command.[91]

Confederate military leaders, believing Hill was burned out because of the large size of his department, decided to divide the area into two commands. The southern district was given to a North Carolina general, while the northern district, of which Roanoke Island was a part, would be turned over to General Wise just before Christmas 1861. Since Wise was a Virginian, the Confederate War Department further decreed that the post should be placed under a newly created department headquartered at Norfolk and placed under the command of General Huger. The change did not affect the complacency that had taken effect.[92]

While the friction between the North Carolina and Georgian troops had been rectified the week before Wise was appointed to the department when Huger ordered the Third Georgia to return to the Norfolk garrison, a new friction, this one between the Virginians and North Carolinians, surfaced. The Georgians were replaced by Colonel John Jordan's Thirty-first North Carolina Infantry, but they were even worse off in regards to supplies, uniform and weapons than the Eighth. Wise was not particularly appreciative of the now all–North Carolinian garrison. Reviewing them, Wise would write, "They were undrilled, unpaid, not sufficiently clothed and quartered and miserably armed." Since the Third Georgia's departure, nothing had been worked on. The lack of Union aggression had made Colonel Shaw complacent. Wise excoriated Shaw. "In a word, the defenses were a sad farce of ignorance and neglect combined, inexcusable in any or all who were responsible for them," he wrote when he landed.[93]

Energetically, Wise dove into his new position with unaccustomed zeal. Arriving on the seventh, Wise ordered Shaw to build a permanent wharf at Weir's Point, near Fort Huger, to expedite the unloading of supplies. He had the North Carolinians commence work on other earthworks and improve those that have been already constructed. To limit the scope of a Union naval assault, Wise ordered pilings to be sunk across the Croatan Sound to hinder the warships' access to the northern part of Roanoke Island. But the area's limitations continued to stall Wise's plans.[94]

Wise's own infantry regiments were delayed in their march from western Virginia, and only a few companies of Lieutenant Colonel Frank P. Anderson's Fifty-ninth Virginia were encamped about the general's headquarters on the Outer Banks at the Nags Head hotel. In the next few weeks, Wise's Forty-sixth Virginia would be trailing in with the rest of Anderson's Fifty-ninth Virginia. Outside of Wilmington, North Carolina, a North Carolina regiment—the Second North Carolina Battalion Infantry, recruited to be part of the Wise Legion—asked Wise to give the orders for it to join the garrison at Roanoke Island. It took some wrangling, but on February 1, Colonel Wharton J. Green's men were ordered to join Wise and embarked on trains for the long, circuitous route to Roanoke Island. These were the positives.[95]

Like Hill before him, Wise found that dealing with Benjamin Huger was an exasperating situation. But unlike Hill, Wise was actually Huger's subordinate, and Wise could only rant against Huger's inaction in private, but it didn't stop him from railing against Huger to anyone who would listen. Wise used his political connections to call attention to his little outpost. After inspecting the island's defenses and assigning Shaw his work list, Wise left for Norfolk to demand support. As he left, two artillery trainers, Captain John S. Taylor and Lieutenant Benjamin Loyall, arrived

General Benjamin Huger was the commander of the Department of Norfolk; because of indifference and difficulty, detractors called him the "barnacle on the Confederacy." *From the Library of Congress.*

to train the newly converted artillerymen who "a week before did not know a ramrod from a lanyard."[96]

Wise presented Huger a shopping list of requests that could have been written by Hill just two months before. Wise demanded 3,000 men on the island with a further 1,500 in support on the beach, trained artillerymen to man the forts' guns, more rifled cannons to cover the ship channel and, most of all, more ammunition, including cannon shells. In all this he would eventually be denied.[97]

While at Norfolk, Wise met the arriving Forty-sixth Virginia Infantry and the missing companies of the Fifty-ninth. In the Forty-sixth was his eldest son, Obediah Jennings Wise, captain of the Norfolk Blues. The father and son had a short reunion, and the regiment was sent on to Roanoke Island, but then the bad news came in droves. The Confederate War Department denied Wise's request for more men for Roanoke Island. His own Third Wise Legion, the Sixtieth Virginia Infantry and the cavalry companies were being diverted to South Carolina to contain the Union advances from Hilton Head and Port Royal. General Huger was retaining Wise's artillerymen and equipment as part of the defenses of Norfolk. The stingy Huger tried to mollify Wise by releasing more rifle cannons but no ammunition. Wise then tried to go over Huger's head and use his vast political power in Virginia politics to get what he needed. For almost a week, Wise pressed the flesh in the government halls at Richmond, but he found himself shut out. Only two more engineer and artillery officers, Lieutenant T.C. Kinney and Captain Schermerhorn, were sent south to the island.[98]

While working the back alleys of power, Wise received continuous reports from Shaw and Navy Commander Lynch. While the situation was depressing, it was at least encouraging that defensive works were coming together. By February 1, both commanders commented that the work was progressing. Lieutenant William Selden, an engineer (having replaced the transferred Dimmock), had improved all the earthworks to accommodate some newly transferred artillery pieces. From the north to the south, the forts were taking shape. Fort Huger, guarding Weir's Point, mounted eight thirty-two-pound smoothbore cannons in an open earthwork called an embrasure, while the two thirty-two-pound smoothbores and two thirty-two-pound rifles flanked the main battery in separated earthworks known as barbettes. Named for the man who unwittingly weakened the island's defenses, its garrison was composed of Captain Gaston D. Cobb's Company I of the Eighth

Formerly the editor of a prestigious Richmond paper, Obediah Jennings Wise made his father's secession course his own and was soon made captain of the "Richmond Blues" militia company. *From Cutchins'* A Famous Command: The Richmond Light Infantry Blues.

North Carolina Infantry turned artillerymen. About 1,200 yards southward was Fort Blanchard, under Lieutenant Isaac Pipkin, and half of Company G of the Thirty-first North Carolina manned the little fort's four thirty-two-pound smoothbores in barbettes. The main fort on the island, the semicircular Fort Bartow, had been expanded to include a newly mounted thirty-two-pound rifle on the fort's left face, while six thirty-two-pound smoothbores overlooked the pilings. Two companies of the Seventeenth North Carolina under Major Gabriel Hill manned the fort. Due to a lack of pilings and a broken pile driver, Lynch and Shaw lamented that there was a 1,700-yard gap in the piling line between Fort Bartow and the mainland defense Fort Forrest, but they had turned to desperate measures of sinking commandeered schooners to fill in the gap. Across the Croatan Sound, the Confederates had abandoned Dimmock's original idea to locate a battery at Robb's Fishery due to the lack of cannons. The earthwork five miles north of Weir's Point was abandoned, and instead, two canalboats were brought into the mud flats just across from Fort Huger. Here, the two boats made a makeshift gun platform with seven thirty-two-pound smoothbores, manned by Captain A.P. White and his Currituck Atlantic Rifles of the Seventeenth North Carolina under the tutelage of Midshipman J.M. Gardner, on loan from Lynch's navy to protect the western end of the obstructing piling line. Near Midgett's Hummock at the end of Shallowback Bay, a two-gun battery of thirty-two-pound smoothbores were manned by Lieutenant William Pulley's Company H of the Thirty-first North Carolina.[99]

The main land defense, the three-gun battery, had seen little improvement. The trees had been cut down for seven hundred yards, but the field had been left untouched since Wright's Georgians had first felled the trees. Due to the high water table, a moat around the earthworks had filled in with brackish water, and the constant rains had eroded the earthwork somewhat. A new crop of tangle foot vines had replaced those that had been removed, and the sawgrass was still sharp. The only difference was that Wise now had planned on meeting the enemy on the shore. To this end, Shaw and Colonel Jordan were told to patrol the island with the remainder of their regiments and the three light artillery pieces. If the Union troops did land, the available Confederate forces were to concentrate on that position and drive the Union forces back to the water's edge. The Eighth and Thirty-first North Carolina Regiments were constantly moving between the southern portion of the island and their camps. The ever increasing Virginians at Nags Head were to gather all available ships and prepare at a moment's notice to ferry the three miles to Roanoke Island and join in the battle.[100]

Wise was pleased with all the activity and complimented the commanders when he returned to the island on February 1. But all this activity had taken its toll on the frail fifty-five-year-old. That night, he went to bed complaining of a fever, and his doctors deduced it was pleurisy, an inflammation of the lungs. The next day, the fever worsened and breathing became difficult. With the general sick and bedridden and an untrusted colonel in charge, now was not the time for a Union attack, but that was exactly what would happen.[101]

5

# "As Though the Sea and Sky Met"

About 130 miles south of Cape Henry, Virginia, is the most dangerous coastline in America: Cape Hatteras. So dangerous is this place where two currents meet crossing over shallow shoals that is known as the "Graveyard of the Atlantic." Many ships have met their doom on its storm-tossed shoreline. Lorenzo Crounse, a writer for the *New York Commercial Advertiser*, described the Hatteras beaches: "At intervals the ribs of half a dozen [wrecks] protruded, a fitting monument to the achievements of an ocean on this terrible coast." The locals had supplemented their meager lives by the bounty of such wrecks, and many houses in the little villages were made wholly from scavenge pieces. From the *Cossack*, Crounse saw one of these local wreckers. "The low beach of Hatteras island stretches along and exhibits a recent wreck high and dry and the tent of some wrecker, who is engaged in dismantling her, close at hand." It was not a kind omen. And heading into this dangerous body of water was the Burnside Expedition with its numerous shallow-draft ships. A well-timed storm could finish Burnside's fleet before it even crossed into North Carolina's shallow sounds.[102]

The voyage began well, as the ships made the best speed southward from Cape Henry into a stiffening south wind. With the wind, the sailing vessels made good speed, soon outdistancing the awkward steamers and overcoming some of Goldsborough's gunboats that were dispatched from other ports. The schooner *Kitty Simpson*, carrying the Fifth Rhode Island, overtook one of these lumbering gunboats on the first night. Closing on it from astern, *Simpson*'s Captain Hepburn hailed the warship. Asked for his ship's name and destination, Hepburn replied, "*Kitty Simpson*—bound south!" Immediately, Hepburn was roundly cursed, the warship beat to quarters and fighting lanterns were lit. Goldsborough's warships had been informed to expect a Confederate privateer in these waters, and the *Kitty Simpson* fit the profile. After a few tense moments as the respective crews stood by their guns (Hepburn's only armament was a four-pound signal cannon), cooler heads prevailed as they closed to visual distance. The warship turned out to be a converted New York City ferryboat mounting four heavy guns. Convinced of the identity of the *Kitty Simpson*, the warship sailed into the ever increasing darkness, leaving the schooner alone.[103]

The next day, Sunday, January 12, the wind picked up and soon turned into a gale. Rounding Cape Hatteras, the *Northerner* carrying the Twenty-first Massachusetts started to wallow in the waves, getting a proper dousing. In the buffeting, the right side engine and boiler support known as a hog brace broke off and fell into the swirling waves. The side-wheeler began to act erratically, and when General Reno went to the bridge to discern the trouble, he found the ship's captain dead drunk. With slurred speech, the captain made his intention to run the ship into the inlet to beat the storm known. Realizing that the captain couldn't navigate in his present condition, Reno had the man forcibly removed from the helm and the ship put into the capable hands of its first mate, who wisely turned the ship back around the cape to better weather the coming storm.[104]

For many of the other ships, the storm's approach just increased their desire to make for the inlet and try to ride it out on the calmer waters of Pamlico Sound inside the Outer Banks. Arriving off the inlet on the thirteenth, David Day, a private in the Twenty-fifth Massachusetts, described the seething froth of churning waves at the inlet:

> *As far as the eye can see, the water is rolling, foaming and dashing over the shoals, throwing its white spray far into the air, as though the sea and sky met…The forces of Heaven are loose and in all their fury, the wind howls, the sea rages, the eternal is here in all his majesty.*

With all this natural violence, passing the inlet at Hatteras seemed unfathomable, but there was more than the horrible weather to comprehend.[105]

The Hatteras Inlet was not the standard inlet. There was not one but two bars to cross. The first one, called "the Swash," was a series of shifting shoals on which the ocean waves crashed with tremendous fury. The ship channel, which changed with the various ocean storms, was purported to be

The storm-tossed Union fleet as viewed by Vizetelly of the *London Illustrated Newspaper. From* London Illustrated Newspaper, *February 12, 1862.*

about nine feet deep, easily passed for most of Burnside's fleet, but there was another potentially more dangerous shoal located behind Hatteras Island. Known by mariners as the "Bulkhead," its shallow water stood as a gateway to the Pamlico Sound and it was supposed to eight feet deep, but the depth charts had not been kept up to date. In between the sandbars, a small harbor of only sixteen square miles existed as a sort of respite for weary mariners before they attempted the Bulkhead. Burnside's and Goldsborough's ships attempted to crowd into this small area to weather the storm. A potential disaster was in the making.[106]

On Monday morning, the thirteenth, Goldsborough arrived at the inlet in the *S.R. Spaulding.* Crossing without any trouble, the flag officer was pleased to find ten of his gunboats riding at anchor inside the inlet. The naval fleet was composed of steamers and converted New York City ferryboats, which drew less than nine feet of water, handpicked for this operation. Later that day, an additional four warships entered the inlet and joined Goldsborough's burgeoning fleet. At this point, Goldsborough's fleet sported thirty-nine guns ranging from thirty-two-pound smoothbores, workhorses of the fleet, to the more modern nine-inch rifles and eighty-pound Parrott rifle cannons, which could far outrange the Confederate pieces. With the new arrivals also came Goldsborough's handpicked tactical commander, Captain Stephen V. Rowan, a fifty-seven-year-old Irish-born curmudgeon with a receding hairline and a bushy mustache. He had been sailing since he was fifteen. He was known for his sharp eye and rapier wit, and at an age when most captains had been retired, Rowan had not only been retained by the navy but also put in active frontline duty. Just not right now. Rowan was ordered to hold his ships in readiness but not to advance into Pamlico Sound until the army transports were all over the Swash. For the time being, the navy could only bob up and down and watch the army ships struggle to make it into the relative safety of the Hatteras harbor.[107]

Trailing behind the *Spaulding* came the *Cossack*, the first of Burnside's transports. Captain Bennett of the *Cossack* was hailed by a pilot coming out to guide the vessel over the bar into the inlet. "What water do you draw?" shouted the pilot over the ever-increasing winds. "Eight feet!" was Bennett's reply. "There is too much sea on the bar for you!" replied the pilot, meaning the ship would ground on the bar. Seeing the *Spaulding* going on alone, Bennett raged against the storm and the pilot, "If she can pass so can we." With the exchange over, Bennett sped over the bar in *Spaulding's* wake, it was the first and last uneventful crossing of the Hatteras bar for Burnside's little fleet.[108]

The largest ship in Burnside's fleet was the *City of New York*, a passenger steamer transformed into a freighter. On the afternoon tide, the captain attempted to pass the ship over the outer bar, but on the approach, the *City of New York* grounded on one of the Outer Banks' notorious shifting shoals and was stuck fast. In the next twenty minutes, the ship was lifted by the waves and smashed on the shoaling fifteen times but still could not work free. The waves crashed against the ship, and every sailor knew that the *City of New York* was in serious trouble. The *City of New York* would last through the tempestuous night, and on the morning of the fourteenth, the boilers flooded and the pumps failed. In desperation, the crew cut down the foremast and smokestack, tossing them into the foam, hoping against hope to lighten the ship and float it off the shoal, but it was a doomed venture. The crew was ordered to abandon the wreck at 8:00 a.m. the next day, and soon thereafter, the *City of New York*, smashed to splinters by the waves, fell to pieces, losing its cargo of artillery shells and equipment. Cape Hatteras's infamous storms had claimed another victim, and many wondered if there would be more among Burnside's little fleet.[109]

Over the next few days, as the storm battered the cape and Burnside's fleet, there were several close calls, but few shipwrecks were as calamitous

The *City of New York* is battered by the Hatteras storms as the fleet watches from a safe distance. *From* Harper's Weekly, *February 15, 1862.*

as the *City of New York*. While passing Cape Hatteras, General Foster aboard the *New Brunswick* had to forego the towed canalboat turned battery *Grapeshot* when the gale hit. The crew of six was rescued before the boat slid below the waves. The gunboat steamer *Zouave*, carrying two companies of the Twenty-fifth Massachusetts, was lining up for its run on the Swash when the ship overran its own anchor and tore a hole in its hull. As *Zouave* began to sink, the captain ran the gunboat on the shoal, and while the deck was soon awash, the men were rescued. Outside of these incidents, the only other casualty was the coal schooner *T.P. Larned*.[110]

This does not mean that accidents did not happen. The steamer *New York*, not to be confused with the wrecked freighter *City of New York*, as many newspapers throughout the North did, suffered from a series of incidents after it crossed into the relative calm behind the Swash. Just after crossing that sandbar, the *New York* collided with the gunboat *Hussar* when the gunboat swung loose of its anchor and smashed in the *New York*'s upper decks. Disentangling *Hussar* tore off part of the aft cabin, exposing the Twenty-fifth Massachusetts's band to the weather. Next, a schooner, sent nearly flying by the strong gale-force wind, slammed headlong into the

*New York*'s wheelhouse. On the fifteenth, a gunboat sideswiped the steamer, causing cosmetic damage to the ship's siding, but the Bay State soldiers' nerves were seriously frayed by the numerous close calls. A drill was added to the Massachusetts troops repertoire when, at a moment's notice, the soldiers were mustered on the deck with oars, boards and muskets to keep any new collisions from happening.[111]

The fifteenth saw an abatement in the storm's fury. The skies lightened, but the wind and waves were still rough and high. The *New Brunswick*, carrying the Tenth Connecticut and General Foster, made its run on the channel on the morning tide after the captain and crew spent the previous ten hours running the ship engine just to maintain their position in the furious storm. After coming to the relatively safe anchorage inside the inlet, the appreciative soldiers cheered the ship's crew and thought about taking a collection for a medal for their service. The storm might have relented, but disasters were still a daily occurrence.[112]

When the Ninth New Jersey arrived outside the inlet aboard the *Ann E. Thompson*, Colonel Joseph Allen and surgeon F.S. Weller decided to report to Burnside personally. Against concerns from the *Thompson*'s captain, Allen and Weller ordered a boat lowered, and wearing overcoats and their swords, the two officers were rowed to the inlet and Burnside's ship. After paying their respects, the boat headed back to the *Thompson* and stuck fast on a shoal. It soon became swamped by the crashing waves. But before any aid could be sent to the floundering rowboat, it flipped. Weller, Allen and one sailor drowned, their bodies washing ashore days later. The New Jerseymen could only watch in disbelief as their officers disappeared below the churning waves.[113]

The drowning of Colonel Allen and Surgeon Weller of the Ninth New Jersey. *From* Frank Leslie's Illustrated Newspaper, *February 15, 1862.*

By the sixteenth, the anchorage was filling up, and room was at a premium. *Cossack* swung on its anchor chain, and for a change, it hit someone else. A brig nearby inflicted terrific damage as its bowsprit tore into the *Cossack*'s four aft staterooms, severely jading the newspapermen's nerves. *Louisiana*, carrying the Sixth New Hampshire, grounded around nightfall, and for the next two days, the soldiers and sailors attempted to lighten the load. But even after removing the men and cargo, the ship was irreparably "hogged" or broken in the middle. The New Hampshiremen were put ashore and added to the garrison of Hatteras, much to their disgust.[114]

That night, another ship, a schooner, sank from the buffeting of the last few days, with water right up to its upper decks. Those in the anchorage looked to the northeast at the Bulkhead and wondered if the worst was behind or in front of them. "If we do not leave this soon, every vessel in the fleet will be disabled or sunk by the combined agency of wind, tide and shoal," wrote one member. As they contemplated their fate, many noticed that bales of hay from the destroyed *City of New York* had grounded on the shoals about the Bulkhead. Was it another bad omen?[115]

A piece of good news arrived on the next day, the eighteenth. The schooner *Scout* arrived at the inlet after being blown nearly seventy miles farther south to Cape Lookout. With only water for two and a half days, the *Scout* had been at sea for over five days. Under the draconian measures instituted by Lieutenant Colonel Thomas Bell of the Fifty-first Pennsylvania, the water was stretched, and the men arrived parched but otherwise healthy. It was a bright moment just as the clouds seem to darken again.[116]

Two days later, a bedraggled bunch of soldiers and some seventeen horses arrived at the Cape, riding along the beach. They were the survivors of the *Pocahontas*, which was carrying a cargo of 123 horses for the generals and their staffs. When the storm had hit, the *Pocahontas* had retreated around the cape as the *Northerner* had done, but the storm was too strong for the little freighter. The thirty-year-old ship was too weak, and its crew ran it as close to the shore as they could get, fifteen miles north of the cape. Tossing the horses out to swim to shore, the crew soon joined them in the seething foam. After spending several days looking for their prized cargo, the crew rounded up the few horses they found and rode or walked down to the point. The horses and men were exhausted. Any officer landing on Roanoke Island would be on foot.[117]

By the twentieth, Burnside ordered his fleet to offload its troops and cargo in an effort to make it easier to cross the Bulkhead. The process of offloading, passing the Bulkhead and reloading the men and material would

The survivors of the horse transport *Pocahontas* suffer through the treacherous surf. *From Frank Leslie's Illustrated Newspaper, February 15, 1862.*

take almost two weeks, losing whatever element of surprise might have been left. Goldsborough, whose fleet took this time to pass to the Pamlico Sound and scout ahead, was surly about the delay. Writing to his wife on the thirtieth, he put his feelings to paper:

> *All my force is still kept hanging by the eyelids awaiting the readiness of General Burnside's branch of the Expedition. The sober truth is ever since the 19th inst. I have been prepared to move. In short, we have failed in nothing whatsoever. All of our detentions have been occasioned by the other branch of the expedition.*

While it seems on face value that this was a correct estimate, it doesn't take into account a piece of good luck that Goldsborough had at this time. To get the ships, naval and army, over the Bulkhead, the fleet needed good stout tugboats, and the five boats that Goldsborough had ordered to join the fleet had not arrived yet. The same weather that had nearly crushed Burnside's fleet had kept these ships in harbor, and it was only by a stretch of luck that the three tugboats ordered to Port Royal, South Carolina, were driven into the Hatteras Inlet on the twenty-first, seeking shelter from a storm. They soon after became part of the Burnside Expedition. For the next two weeks, the tugboats *Phoenix*, *Patuxent* and *Pilot Boy* would be doing yeoman service for the fleet.[118]

In order to expedite the Bulkhead crossing, Goldsborough resorted to a dangerous scheme. Knowing that the water level over the Bulkhead was less than over the Swash and seeing how much trouble the fleet had crossing it, Goldsborough sent the steamer USS *Stars and Stripes* across the Bulkhead and, once over, anchored it on the bar. He ordered the little steamer then to reverse engines and to continue until it had returned to the anchorage side of the Bulkhead. In this manner the steamer would have dug a channel through the sandbar. The USS *Lockwood* was also detached to aid the *Stars and Stripes* in improving the channel. After two days of hard toil and strain on the engines, the channel was cut on the twentieth. The channel improved the depth to eight feet, allowing most of the fleet to pass with relative ease, but the damage to the *Stars and Stripes* was substantial. In the process of cutting the channel, sand had worked up into the engine, tearing up moving parts. *Stars and Stripes* was out of commission for several days as its engineer disassembled the motor, cleared the sand out and then reassembled the same, a time-consuming but necessary development.[119]

The fleet began the slow process of crossing the Bulkhead and, by the twenty-second, had only just started when another nor'easter storm raged on the Outer Banks. The gale slammed the ships together, but the only thing destroyed was the men's nerves. The *Northerner*, catching the wind and dragging its anchors, lashed itself to a couple of schooners to stop from running ashore. Italian-born Lieutenant Colonel Maggi oversaw the lashings, complimenting his men for their alacrity, when one of the schooner's captains appeared with a boarding axe and began cutting the lashings. Maggi flew into a storm of oaths, some in English and others in Italian, and drawing his pistol, he threatened to kill the captain on the spot. Angered by the military interloper, the schooner captain launched into epithets on Maggi's Italian birth. Calling him an organ grinder, the captain struck a nerve. Maggi called for a file of men to train their rifles on the captain and shoot him if he made a move. The captain withdrew to his cabin, mumbling under his breath, but above decks, the Massachusetts men truly felt vindicated in having chosen Maggi for their commander.[120]

When the storm hit the Twenty-fourth Massachusetts, it was ashore near the two forts of Hatteras and Clark. The winds and waves forced it to first move its tents and then abandon its camp altogether. Marching six miles through surf and rain to safer, higher ground, the men found only their knapsacks kept them upright, and they crowded into an old shanty near Fort Clark. After returning to camp, the Twenty-fourth found that it had accidentally moved its camp in a cemetery, and the stench was miserable. For the men, their weeklong stay on Hatteras was a hell of water, stench and sand, and when the men would curse one another, instead of "Go to hell!" they shouted, "Go to Hatteras!" Everyone on the expedition could relate.[121]

The second storm ended on the twenty-fourth, and the water-starved soldiers lapped up the heavy rain it had produced. So poor were the water supplies that before the storm, the men had been drinking desalinated water from the ships' boilers or the stinking water stored in rotting whiskey barrels. The rest of the supplies were barely better. One patriot believed they could stomach the salty meat and a weevily biscuit for the Union, but bad water was too much.[122]

With all this difficulty, the army moved over the Bulkhead, but some ships just could not make it due to depth. The *Ann E. Thompson* was just too heavy. The Ninth New Jersey was put on the *Kitty Simpson* after the Sixth New Hampshire had been put ashore to supplement the Hatteras garrison. The *Guerilla*, the former slave ship, drew too much water as well, so the five companies of the Twenty-seventh Massachusetts Infantry were put on the hospital ship *Recruit*. The Eighty-ninth New York was likewise removed to join the garrison at Hatteras when the *Aracan* proved to draw too much water to operate in the sound.[123]

All of this delay did not go unnoticed by the Confederates. Having waited for the blow to fall ever since the twelfth, Confederate forces were a little impatient when a week passed, then another and even another before there was any noticeable activity. Some saw the two nor'easter storms as God's providence. "God in his mercy has sent the winds to war against our enemies and has humbled their haughty pride," wrote one North Carolina lawyer. Others saw that the nature of North Carolina's coastline was an enemy for Burnside more potent than any with shot or shell. The *Richmond Examiner* wrote on February 4 that "nature has prepared a defense for fertile Eastern North Carolina against invasion." Confederates railed in the press against the "Burnside Armada," which they envisioned, like Spain's armada, had been smashed on Hatteras's sandy shoals. "The highest achievement it can accomplish will be that of taking care of itself," continued the *Examiner*'s editor, "as an aggressive demonstration it is pitiful." The day after the *Examiner* condemned Burnside's fleet to an ignominious end on North Carolina's shoaled coastline, the fleet of sixty-five ships with twelve thousand soldiers aboard hauled anchor and set a course for Roanoke Island. There was no going back.[124]

# 6

# "So Here We Go for a Trip Up the Sound, Probably for Roanoke Island"

The last weeks in January saw some of Burnside's late arrivals finally make an appearance. The *Colonel Slattery*, carrying Burnside's Signal Corps detachment, arrived on the twenty-eighth. Since being lost in the fog bank around Annapolis in the beginning of the voyage, the *Slattery* had been playing catch-up. Arriving at Fort Monroe on the sixteenth, the ship missed the expedition by nearly four days. While passing down the coast, just missing the first storm, the schooner actually came within sight of the Cape Hatteras Lighthouse when the paranoid ship's captain spied a sailing vessel heading for them. Determining it to be a Rebel privateer, he changed course and put out to sea, in an attempt to lose the Rebels in deep water. The ensuing delay only angered the army officers, who demanded he return to the inlet. They arrived at the inlet on the twenty-second just as the second storm hit. While at anchor, the storm tossed the ship, dragging it on anchor and throwing the cargo and men about. Water started to come over the deck, and the ship was forced to head for deep water to ride out the storm. As if their troubles weren't enough, the Signal Corpsmen soon smelled smoke, only to find the ship's captain drunk and stocking his cabin stove until it was glowing. At this most dangerous moment, the army men put the captain in the hold, put the fire out and had the first mate take over the ship. Just then, their luck turned. The sun came out, and although they were four hundred miles from the inlet, they found a favoring breeze that brought them back in quick time. Finally, on January 28, the *Colonel Slattery* reunited with the fleet.[125]

The ship that the *Colonel Slattery*'s captain might have seen was the luckless *John Trucks*. On the twenty-third, the long-suffering *John Trucks* finally arrived with the Fifty-third New York. After being left stuck fast on the Chesapeake Bay shoal two weeks before, the *John Trucks* too had been playing catch-up with the rest of the fleet. It just missed the fleet at Hampton Roads when it became stuck again on a sandbar. Then, the nor'easter that nearly wrecked the fleet turned the *Trucks* back into Hampton Roads. The trip down had been abysmal. Crowded conditions and poor sanitary features soon meant the Zouaves were sick and crawling with lice and other vermin. Their officers had locked themselves from the men, staying in the aft cabins, and when they did deign to come out of their cabins, it only led to more strife. On one occasion, while a soldier was grooming his moustache he was justly proud of, D'Epineuil displayed the kind of reaction that confirmed de Monteil's accusations that the commanding officer was crazy. D'Epineuil, seeing the man and his moustache, screamed at him, decrying the moustache as a poor example of facial hair. He then grabbed both ends of the man's moustache and tore them off. As the poor soldier screamed in pain, D'Epineuil offered his opinion on any other moustaches. On a another part of the trip, D'Epineuil harangued the men that he was, as a colonel, akin to their father but then rambled on for nearly two hours in an incomprehensible diatribe. When Burnside viewed the *John Trucks*, many of the men had burned their uniforms and were wrapped up in blankets to cover up their nakedness. It was obvious that D'Epineuil's unit was useless. Burnside ordered the *John Trucks* back to Annapolis, ostensibly due to the lack of shallow draft boats to carry the Zouave regiment, but in reality, Burnside wanted to wash his hands of the Fifty-third New York. The hapless Zouaves were soon broken up, with two of the companies being parceled out to other New York regiments, while the rest of the unit was unceremoniously mustered out, officers included.[126]

Ironically, Burnside had just added another New York Zouave unit to his expedition. Hawkins's Zouaves had been on Hatteras since it fell to Union forces in August. Since then, Hawkins's men had survived a Confederate attack, but mostly boredom, winter storms and sand fleas. The rough-and-tumble Zouaves were from New York City and the surrounding areas. They wore a uniform different in many respects to the faded glory of the Fifty-third New York. Recruited early in the war, the Ninth's Zouave uniform was quickly made in the expectation of a short war. Their fezzes were red with blue tassels, while the dark blue short jackets had red trim but no motif designs, called tombeauxs. Their dark blue vests were piped in light blue trim while their sashes were light blue as well. Their trousers were more like the common soldiers' but dark blue as well and had red wool stripes down the side. Gaiters were white canvass or black leather to deal with the sharp cacti of the Outer Banks. They were tough, no-nonsense men who viewed themselves as veterans, having fought in some minor skirmishes and taken the inlet that summer, among Burnside's green recruits. Nothing they had experienced had prepared them for what was to come. But knowing that the terrain and their fighting style made them important to the mission, they joined the fleet on the February 3. They joined General Parke's Third Brigade, replacing the Sixth New Hampshire and Eighty-ninth New York. They were crowded aboard the stern paddle-wheeler transport *Union*, which, being so ungainly, was rechristened by the Zouaves as the "Wheelbarrow." Two companies were placed on board the steam gunboat *Virginia*, Parke's flagship for the voyage.[127]

The Ninth's colonel had spent most of the winter in front of court-martials or carrying the plan to use the Hatteras post as a jumping-off point for a North Carolina campaign, but he had also been gathering information. Hawkins had secreted some of his men in civilian clothing on to Roanoke Island, where they observed the Confederates fortifying the island, but it was the slaves who fished the waters or had fled their masters to Hatteras who were the best sources. "If you need information, ask the negro," was a Hawkins proverb, and from them, he found out most of what he knew. Hawkins informed Burnside that the Confederate garrison had established martial law on the island, forcing white fishermen to refrain from their occupation. It was felt that locals would give fish and information to Union troops at Hatteras. This situation angered many of the locals, who had no other way to make a living, but others sidestepped the law and sent their slaves out to do the same thing. Hawkins's sources told Burnside that there were four major forts on the island and camps for upward of ten thousand men but that they were not filled yet. His sources also gave him a pretty good layout of the island itself, but he needed a harbor. That information came in the form of young Thomas Robinson, a fifteen-year-old slave escapee who arrived just as Burnside was planning his next part of the campaign.[128]

Many slaves had taken advantage of the Union occupation of Hatteras to seek their freedom. One slave family arrived with fifteen children in tow. They were interviewed and then processed to a camp located just outside the walls of Fort Clark, called Hotel d'Afrique. For the week before Burnside's departure, every person arriving from the north was carefully screened for information. Most were useless, but when Robinson and his brother arrived in a small sailing vessel, known locally as a "cooner," they brought with them detailed information about the island. Robinson was the slave of J.M. Daniel, who had rented the boy out to the Confederate forces as a laborer. Robinson had been up and down the length of the island and was smart enough to remember all the gun positions and layouts of the forts. He had even been to the Confederate camps and knew roughly how many troops were in the area. Overhearing officers talking, Robinson even knew that some of the Wise Legion was encamped at Nags Head across Roanoke Sound, waiting to be utilized. Interviewed on Hatteras Island, he was brought to Burnside's attention and soon became privy to all the general's planning meetings and stayed in the same ship's cabin as the general on the voyage to Roanoke Island.[129]

Hawkins's men brought with them another former slave whose hidden talent would aide the navy. "Old" Benjamin Tillett was a tall, strong inland sailor who had abandoned his master and family in a ship he stole during a particularly nasty Outer Banks nor'easter. Joining the Ninth New York, Tillett piloted many of Hawkins's clandestine operations and, because of his innate knowledge of the Pamlico Sound, was loaned to the navy to pilot the ships through the difficult and tight ship channel.[130]

By February 4, Burnside had informed Goldsborough that the army was ready to sail, and on the fifth, the ships made ready to sail. Sails were unfurled and steamers warmed up their boilers as thick black smoke rose from their stacks. The sun shone, and the sky seemed tranquil for the first time in a month. "The clink of the windlass is heard on all the boats, hoisting up their anchors so here we go for a trip up the sound, probably for Roanoke Island," wrote the Twenty-fifth Massachusetts's David Day. It reminded many of the departure from Annapolis, and to cap it off, Burnside, aboard the little *Picket*, changed vessels and boarded the *S.R. Spaulding* to cheers from the army and navy. During the storms, the unwell general had been seen everywhere by everyone. He had calmed the nerves of the soldiers as the *Picket* sped around the harbor. Now, after a week of relative relaxation, Burnside looked forward to the coming fight.[131]

The voyage that first day was peaceful. The naval warships led three separate columns northward, followed by the army gunboats in a supportive role, and farther down the sound were the transports. After passing about fifty miles from Hatteras and less than ten miles from Roanoke Island, Goldsborough rallied his fleet outside a small harbor on the North Carolina mainland called Stumpy Point. Most of the ships arrived in the dimming twilight and marveled at the scenery. The ships, nearly seventy, seemed an unstoppable armada, especially after getting this deep in enemy territory

After a month of wrecks in Hatteras storms, Burnside's fleet passes the Marsh Islands on February 7, 1862. *From* Frank Leslie's Illustrated Newspaper, *March 8, 1862.*

One of Goldsborough's gunboats was the converted New York ferryboat *Commodore Perry*. *From the National Archives.*

with no real threat. Maybe the campaign would be as easy as it had been advertised. Then, the rain, which seemed to be timed with the expedition's arrival in North Carolina, started again, ending the romance of a quick war and dry bedding.[132]

Three steam tugs took up the night's picket duties by steaming up to a chain of swampy island known locally only as the Marshes. Steaming up to them, Goldsborough hoped to determine if the Confederates had closed the channel through or placed a battery on the islands that might delay the attack. They arrived just as the rain abated and only saw the lights of the Confederate ship CSS *Appomattox* as it chugged back up the sound toward the Confederate defense. There were no defenses and no Confederate picket ship waiting, which was good news for the three tugs, as Goldsborough had, in his opening gambit, sent unarmed ships to reconnoiter the position. The rain soon enveloped the fleet again and lasted until the next sunrise.[133]

After spending a fretful day waiting for a Union attack that failed to materialize, many of the Confederate navy's officers were exhausted. The captains of the understrength fleet knew what was before them and how their army comrades called them derisively the "Mosquito Fleet," small and annoying. Lynch and his men had aided the infantrymen turned artillerymen ashore and had been running back and forth responding to Wise's calls for more supplies, pilings and scows to sink behind the pilings, filling in the obstruction. Late that night, after seeing to his men's food and bedding, Captain William Parker, captain of the CSS *Beaufort*, went aboard Flag Officer Lynch's flagship, CSS *Sea Bird*, to confer with his commander. Lynch had sent word that he wanted to see Parker, another experienced former United States naval officer, but when Parker did not arrive, Lynch chalked it up to exhaustion and prepared for bed himself. Surprised at Parker's arrival, Lynch met him in his cabin in a dressing gown and reading *Ivanhoe*. Parker and Lynch were realists. "We talked for a long time of what the next day would probably bring forth, and our plans for defense etc. We neither of us believed that we would be successful," recalled Parker. The odds were just too much. "Ten thousand men to our two thousand on land and nineteen vessels and 54 guns to our eight vessels with 9 guns on the water," Parker commented. Lynch and Parker sat overwhelmed by the prospect of the hopelessness of the situation, and somehow the subject was changed to literature. That topic, and Lynch's expedition to the Dead Sea in the 1840s, soon consumed the evening, and when the watches switched at midnight, the two men were shocked at the lateness of the hour. Seeing Parker to his gig, Lynch's parting sounded more like a premonition. "Ah! If we could only hope for success, but come again when you can," called Lynch after Parker. A disturbed but resolute Parker headed back into the inky darkness, wondering if they would survive the coming battle.[134]

# "Every Man Is Expected to Do His Duty"

Thursday, February 7, dawned warm and muggy for February, and as the day before, after breakfast, the ships engines were brought to life, pumping out black smoke from their stacks, while sailing vessels loosened their ties, spilling out their sails to catch the morning wind. The fleet stirred and, in the sunshine, began to head for the Marsh Island. The USS *Underwriter* led the fleet, its guns primed and ready for actions.[135]

North of the Marsh Islands, the new watch of the CSS *Curlew* had just come on duty and took their positions. Captain Thomas Hunter scanned the channels with his glass and soon caught sight of the *Underwriter* coming through the Marsh Islands. Behind *Underwriter*, Hunter saw the rest of the naval gunboats chugging to catch up. Outgunned, Hunter quickly ordered the *Curlew* to withdraw back to the Confederate fleet. The naval battle of Roanoke Island had begun.[136]

At 9:00 a.m., the rest of the Union fleet fell into two lines behind the *Underwriter*, moving resolutely through the Marsh Islands. As with the advance from Hatteras, the fleet moved in three columns, with the naval gunboats in the lead. Behind them came Hazard's army gunboats, except for two ships left to corral the transports. The transports, with nearly thirteen thousand infantrymen crowding the ships' decks for a view of the approaching action, soon anchored again just behind the Marsh Islands, awaiting the outcome of the bombardment.[137]

An hour and a half later, the Confederate navy announced the Union fleet's arrival when the CSS *Sea Bird* fired its forward gun from behind the obstruction line. The gun was merely a signal to the rest of the Confederates, as the *Underwriter* was well out of range, but immediately, the island was a bustle of activity. Guns were manned and primed, ready for action. The picket ship CSS *Curlew*, churning the blue water, soon passed the piling line and took its position at the end of Lynch's line, having performed its duty admirably. The Confederates were ready for battle.[138]

Completing its transit of the Marsh Islands, the *Underwriter* began to hug Roanoke Island's western coastline, hoping to spot any hidden shore batteries that Union informants had missed. Passing Sand Point, about two and a half miles south of Fort Bartow, the *Underwriter*'s captain, Lieutenant Commander W.V. Jefferies, hoisted the all-clear signal, and the U.S. gunboats followed him in quick succession. Half an hour later, at 11:00 a.m., Goldsborough, in the *Philadelphia*, located between the naval forces and the transports, hoisted his signal flags that spelled Admiral Lord Nelson's famous order to his men at Trafalgar: "This country expects every man to do his duty." The mood among the sailors was electric, and cheering soon broke out on all the fleet's ships. Even the troops crammed on the transports eight miles behind the gunboats cheered as soon as it was explained to them what the little flags meant.[139]

By 11:30 a.m., the gunboats under Goldsborough's Irishman, Rowan, began to open fire on their targets. Shells began to rain down on Fort Bartow, and by 12:00 p.m., they were being pummeled. At the obstruction line, Lynch fired a few salvos and then began to peel away to the north end of the island in an attempt to goad the Union gunboats to follow him. It was hoped that the heavier draft Union gunboats would take the bait and either become immobilized on the barrier or, in crossing it, be severely damaged in the crossfire of the four forts. In this, he was disappointed. Rowan ordered his captains to concentrate their fire and attention on the fort and forego the departing steamers.[140]

Aboard the *S.R. Spaulding*, Burnside viewed the bombardment with a bit of reserve. If the navy could not silence the battery, then what would become of his landing? Had they gone all the way to be stopped by sand and pilings? Already the fire from the fort had slackened, but it was stubbornly responding with the occasional round. Burnside saw that the fire wasn't all one-sided. Some of the gunboats were taking punishment from Confederate fire. He ordered Hazard's gunboats to join the navy bombardment and waited patiently for a sign of weakness on the Rebels' part. While he pondered his next move, the *Cadet* with Ferrero's Fifty-first New York pulled alongside, cheering. Burnside pulled down his glasses and led his men in a set of cheers.[141]

Based on a drawing by a participant, the Union fleet bombards Fort Bartow. *From* Frank Leslie's Illustrated Newspaper, *March 8, 1862.*

Fort Bartow's response was limited, not due to the bombardment but in spite of it. Bartow's nine guns stood ready that morning, as they had been when they were first installed, but as they were, only three of the guns were even placed in a position to return the Union fire. The other six guns, including a rifled piece, were situated in such a way as to fire on ships crossing the obstruction line. With Union warships remaining south of the line, the guns stood idly by, waiting for their chance. For that matter, so poorly sited were all the other forts that not one of the other gun positions could aid in the battle. Forts Huger's and Blanchard's guns were out of range, and Fort Forrest's pieces could only just reach the main shipping channel, far short of most of the Union gunboats, which were still hugging the island's shore. To complicate Bartow's response even more, at 12:30 p.m., the rifled gun exploded, blowing it off its carriage and killing two men and wounding another. Only two other gunners were wounded by the mass volume of Union iron.[142]

Being limited in their response did not mean Major Hill's gunners were kowtowed—far from it. Nearly thirty rounds from the fort struck the wooden fleet. The USS *Louisiana* took a shot to its decking early in the fight. It passed through half-inch iron plating and crashed through the bulkhead above the magazine and then entered a coal bunker and detonated, setting the ship aflame. The concussion from the shell blew open all the closed hatchway doors. Captain Alexander Murray was forced to pull the ship out of the fight while his brave sailors put the blaze out. He would return to the fight later, but it was a scary moment. If the shell had only detonated a few seconds earlier, the ensuing explosion in the *Louisiana*'s powder magazine would have atomized the steamer. The USS *J.N. Seymour*, a sailing gunboat, took a cannonball into the deck, decapitating one sailor. In the early part of the fight, the *Hunchback* closed in on the fort to make its shots count. After taking six incidental rounds, the crew's luck ran out at 3:30 p.m. when one round damaged the engine, carrying away one of the cylinder guide rods and the spring bow. Another skipped across the Croatan Sound and plowed through the ship's hull right at the waterline. Injured, Lieutenant E.R. Colhoun's gunners stuck by their guns, firing over three hundred rounds at the Confederates.[143]

Some of the Union warships were just unlucky. The shoals near Roanoke Island are as imperceptible as those at Hatteras, and several Union ships ran aground during the fighting. The *Stars and Stripes*, the little steam gunboat that had opened the channel across the Bulkhead, was in action for six hours, two of them aground on a sandbar underneath the guns of Fort Bartow. Nearly pulverized by the accurate gunners, the plucky little gunboat eventually limped away, guns still blazing away defiantly.[144]

Army gunboats were not beyond these nautical failings. The *Ranger* and *Chasseur* both ran aground, taking several hits while stuck fast; only the fast actions of the tug *Tempest* saved the gunboats. The *Tempest*, under fire, towed both ships away from the obstruction line, where the gunboats tangled with Fort Forrest. No sooner had the *Tempest* cleared the army boats than *Ranger*, returning to the fight, grounded again. Still recovering from the heavy lifting

After performing heroic feats to get the fleet over the bar, the various tugboats continued to carry out duties far above their simple tasks. Here, the *Tempest* saves the *Chasseur*. *From* Frank Leslie's Illustrated Newspaper, *March 8, 1862.*

the tugboats had done getting the fleet over the Bulkhead the week before, the little tugboats once again earned the respect of the entire fleet.[145]

The little gunboat *Hetzel* suffered from a combination of bad luck and good gunnery from Fort Bartow. Taking up its post bombarding the fort, the ship expended over one hundred rounds but not before a thirty-two-pound solid shot from the fort crushed the siding of the ship. About an hour later, the Confederate gunners scored another hit on the *Hetzel* when a shell detonated above the *Hetzel*'s deck, killing Master's Mate Charles Harris. After fixing the damage and returning to its place in the line, the *Hetzel* was hit by misfortune. The eighty-pounder Parrott gun on the aft deck exploded, horribly wounding the crew of six. The gun split into three pieces, with two pieces falling harmlessly into the sound or on the deck, but the third piece, weighing one thousand pounds, smashed through the deck and into the aft magazine. The powder took light, and only the quick response from the crew saved the ship from disaster.[146]

Lieutenant Charles Flusser, commanding the converted ferryboat *Commodore Perry*, brought his ship in close to make full use of his nine-inch smoothbore guns. Flusser, seeing his shells delayed in exploding, made the adjustments to the fuse personally, cutting them down with his own pen knife. With the reworked fuses, the *Commodore Perry*'s shells began to damage the fort severely. Pushing closer, Flusser became hung up on a sandbar. In quick succession, the Confederate cannoneers responded with eight hits. One hit the hurricane deck near where the pilothouse was, tearing away the guardrail. Then the flagstaff was snapped by a passing shot. Next, another solid shot splintered part of the bulwark, wounding a volunteer from the Fourth Rhode Island infantry. Then, two rounds slammed into the ship below the waterline, quickly followed by two more just above the same area. The last round hit the upper decking as the *Perry* pulled free from the bank. A well-timed shell or hot shot would have destroyed the *Perry*, but fortunately, the Confederates had few of either. At 1:00 p.m., the fort's flagpole was blown apart by one of Flusser's shells, and soon after, an oily black fire began to appear from the fort's barracks behind the earthwork. A cry rose up from the Union forces, believing the fort was faltering under the heavy bombardment.[147]

Inside the fort, Hill's gunners, now under the eye of Colonel Shaw, were doing their best. Return fire was limited in an effort to save the sparse ammunition. Those rounds that were fired were carefully aimed, doing fearful damage and showing the drill that Captain Taylor and Major Hill put them through was paying dividends. Under such conditions, the men were surprisingly upbeat. When the flagpole was shattered by the bombardment, Private William C. Dawson from Pasquotank County's State Guards rushed forward and planted the company's flag on the sandy battlements. Through their glasses, the Union officers, appreciating the bravery, blew their whistles as tokens of respect. Dawson, after planting the flag, doffed his cap and then returned to his piece. Behind the embankments, Dawson's bravery was cheered by his comrades.[148]

When the flag came down, Burnside, on the *Spaulding*, thought that was the moment his troops needed to land. "That battery is about silenced; I will take these troops and land," he mentioned to his staff. But then Dawson planting his small flag and a defiant gun report convinced him otherwise. The landings would have to wait a bit longer.[149]

Behind the fort, the wooden barracks that had been home to the Seventeenth North Carolina since September caught fire. The pine boards soon crackled and produced a thick, oily smoke, and the flames rose in a column fifty feet high. With all the men tied fast to their cannons, no one except one of the black servants was available to save the companies' equipment. Through the heavy bombardment and with shells crashing among the camp buildings, this unnamed slave attempted to save what he could. Cooking implements, clothing and some accoutrements were saved in this manner, but over two hundred rifles and ammunition was lost. The fire would burn well into the night, and on the morning of the eighth, a smoldering pall still hung over the area.[150]

After trying most of the beginning of the battle to lure the Union gunboats farther north, Flag Officer Lynch realized the Union navy had not taken his bait. Seeing the plume of smoke rising above Fort Bartow, Lynch ordered his fleet into the fight to take some of the pressure off the army gunners. Lynch had been forced to make some deletions to his fleet before he headed southward. The *Appomattox* had been sent in the morning to get more shells and had not been recalled. The schooner *Black Warrior* was too unwieldy, and its guns were too light to battle with the Union gunboats, so it remained at the north end near Fort Huger overlooking the fight. As the remaining six gunboats steamed southward, they passed a tender and some schooners carrying Confederate reinforcements to bolster the island's garrison. They cheered the grim Confederates, who believed the odds were not in their favor of returning.[151]

Over on Nags Head, General Wise was doing everything he could to aid Shaw from his sickbed. Kept constantly aware of the developing situation, Wise ordered Lieutenant Colonel Frank Anderson, with eight companies of the Fifty-ninth Virginia and two companies of the Forty-sixth Virginia, about 450 men, to reinforce the island as soon as the first naval discharges were heard. Arriving at about 1:30 p.m., Anderson's men waded in to shore because of the lack of wharves at Weir's Point and headed down to the three-gun battery at the center of the island. Wise then ordered Major Henry Fry to mobilize the five companies of the Forty-sixth Virginia, or 150 men, to stand ready to join the garrison. This left Wise with a scant 200 men to defend Nags Head if the Union landed on the beaches. With these reinforcements and the expected arrival of Colonel J. Wharton Green's Second North Carolina Battalion any day, the Confederate army seemed prepared for a land battle. It was all the sickly general could do.[152]

As Lynch's gunboats fired up their engines and headed south, their black plumes drew unwarranted attention. Several Union gunboats changed from punishing Fort Bartow, now on fire, to dealing with the new threat of Confederate ships. The Confederate fleet began to take heavy fire as it steamed along the obstruction line. At about 2:00 p.m., the CSS *Forrest* was struck so hard its propeller was disabled. Another shell exploded over the decks, cutting Lieutenant James L. Hoole across the head. Bleeding profusely, Hoole pointed his crippled ship to the mainland coast south of Fort Forrest. Run aground, Hoole and his artillerists soon joined Fort Forrest army gunners and attempted to keep up the fight, but the *Forrest* was out of action. After thirty minutes in action, Lynch turned his fleet northward again to lick his wounds, his raid barely influencing the Union bombardment at all.[153]

It was now about 3:00 p.m., and with the fort's fire diminished and Lynch's fleet in retreat, Burnside decided to prepare for his troops' landing. Just before heading over to the *Philadelphia* for a conference with Commodore Goldsborough, Burnside dispatched his topographical engineer, Lieutenant William Andrews of the Ninth New York, and six soldiers from the Fifth Rhode Island in a gig to take soundings of the landing point, Ashby's Harbor. Ever since the fleet sailed north from Hatteras, Burnside had pored over maps of Roanoke Island and, with Thomas Robinson providing much more detailed information, had concocted his plan. There were only two suitable landing places on the island south of the obstruction line: Pugh's and Ashby's Landings. Robinson counselled for Ashby's, and Burnside concurred. It was located about two miles south of Fort Bartow and near to the main north–south road granting access to the middle of the island. Pugh's, on the other hand, was located near the southern extremity of the island five miles away, across nearly impassable swamps and open to ambush from the three-gun battery. If Burnside could get his men ashore at Ashby's Harbor, he would then be that much closer to dryer ground and the Confederate forces. Ashby's it was, and so that was where Andrews and his boat were heading as the weak winter sun dully tried to warm up the air.[154]

Before he had been stricken with pleurisy, Wise had made it vitally important to Shaw and Jordan to oppose any infantry landing on the beach. If the Confederates could throw the Union forces back into the water, then the Union might retreat, believing the island too heavily defended. This ruse would hide the actual Confederate numbers. The only circumstance where Wise believed the troops should withdraw would be when and if their field artillery was compromised and in danger of falling to the enemy—then and only then would the troops be ordered to fall back on the three-gun battery.[155]

Respecting Wise's advice, Shaw had cleared the camps of nearly all the unassigned men. Jordan's Thirty-first North Carolina and two of the three light guns marched out of the three-gun battery and established his command at Ashby's Landing. Farther south, Shaw's Eighth North Carolina, with the remaining gun under Major George Williamson, spent the early morning hours of the sixth in and about Pugh's Landing. When the Union transports started to pass the Marsh Islands, Shaw, who had joined Williamson from Fort Bartow, carefully discerned their path. His suspicions were confirmed when the transports passed Pugh's without slowing. The Union were going to land at Ashby's.[156]

Ashby's Harbor is a broad half-moon, shallow bay. At the south end of the bay lay Captain Solomon Ashby's farm. A former sea captain, Ashby had had the largest number of slaves on Roanoke Island, thirty-five, before the war, but many were too young to do the demanding fishing work. The farm was broad and bordered a sluggish stream that bisected the harbor. North of the creek was Thomas Hayman's home, a small little farmhouse and outbuildings surrounded by an appreciable cornfield. The little creek curved behind Hayman's farm fields to the north, and beyond it were thick, swampy woods.[157]

Williamson's men were ordered to make their best speed to the three-gun battery, and they passed Jordan's men just before 3:00 p.m. Here, Shaw rejoined Jordan. Informed that the Union was going to test him first, Jordan set up his men about half a mile from Captain Ashby's house and anchored on the main road. Jordan sent Captain Edward R. Liles with a picket force of twenty-five men ahead of his main line. Reminding Jordan to resist the landing, Shaw soon left to oversee the defenses at the three-gun battery.[158]

Lieutenant Andrews and his reconnaissance party are fired upon. *From* Frank Leslie's Illustrated Newspaper, *April 5, 1862.*

Jordan's men crouched in the tall swamp grass and looked out into Croatan Sound. It was filled with more ships than many of them had ever seen, and with the gunboats pounding Fort Bartow, many must have wondered if stopping the Union was an impossible situation. It must have been an awesome sight.

Thirty minutes after they left the fleet, Andrews and his gig were spotted by Captain Liles's men. The Unionists were taking soundings and then eventually landed ashore. Liles moved his men through the swamp grass stealthily, hoping to capture the reconnoitering party without a shot, but two overeager North Carolinians blew the plan when they broke cover by cheering and whooping.[159] Surprised, Andrews and his men fled back to their boat and pushed off. Now beyond capture, Liles ordered his men to shoot into the boat. A round smashed into one of the oars and another hit Private Charles Vail in the jaw, exiting his cheek. Before another volley could be loosed, the Union boat had retreated out of range. Frustrated, Liles and his men slinked back into the swamp grass.

Andrews's boat made directly for the *Philadelphia*, where he made his report to Burnside. Ashby's Harbor was deep enough for their purposes, and while it was guarded, Andrews felt that the resistance was minimal. Even Private Vail was positive. Being sewed up by the doctors, Vail joked that his mouth was spoiled for hardtack.

It was then agreed that the landing would go forward as planned, and the signal flag was raised on the *Philadelphia*'s bridge. An excited cry, which for a moment drowned out the barrage, burst from the infantry-crowded transports, and the long-awaited landing began.[160]

8

# "If I Can Get Two Thousand Men Ashore I Am All Right"

Coming ashore on an occupied area had never before been attempted by the United States military. Under normal conditions, the landing force selected a secluded or otherwise empty zone, and while the naval bombardment occupied the attention of the enemy, the landings commenced without molestation. From the secured beachhead, the forces advanced on the enemy, closing the noose in a siege or a proper battle. Burnside's men were entering new territory when the landing signal flag was hoisted on the *Philadelphia*. Planning was very important, and during the last week of January, that is exactly what Burnside and his generals had done when they were sequestered in his cabin aboard the *Picket*. "If I can get two thousand men ashore I am all right," Burnside commented when he first contemplated his landings, about the time he dispatched Andrews and his crew. For the plan to succeed, everything had to go off without a hitch. A failing in any part of the plan could result in disaster.[161]

With his engineering acumen, Foster had laid out the plans. The troops would land in three waves, each brigade landing one-third of its men in each wave. On the first wave Foster and his men were scheduled to land first with Reno in support. Parke would reinforce the landing with his detachment about twenty minutes later. The light draft tugboats would drag the nearly sixty rowboats toward the shore, and when within fifty feet, the tugboats would reverse engines and slingshot the rowboats into the shoreline. The tugboats would get as far in to shore as possible and then disgorging their charges, pick up the rowboats and do it all again. If all went well nearly

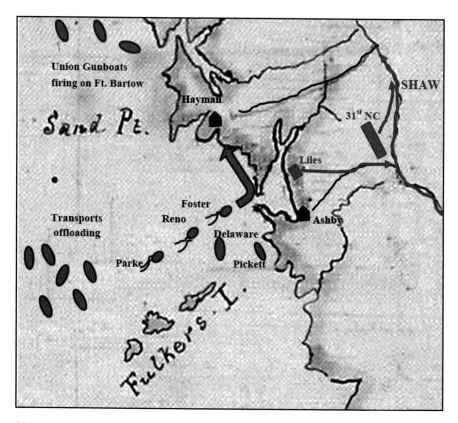

Union landings, February 7, 1862.

four thousand men would be ashore in a matter of minutes. Foster felt he had planned for every circumstance—he even had a waiting gunboat in case of enemy resistance on the beach—but how the green troops would react if they came under fire while on the water was something no one could predict.[162]

Each brigadier had selected one of the proven tugboats to act as his lead ship. Foster chose the *Pilot Boy*, Reno had the *Patuxent* and Parke would embark on the *Phoenix*; each tug was loaded with as many men as it could fit, some fitting up to five hundred men. The tugs came to stop near the transports now located in Croatan Sound; behind each tug, two ropes were tied off and dragged in the water. A U.S. flag flying from each ship's foremast was the signal for the transports to load the troops into the landing boats; rowboats, ship's gigs, even the rubber pontoon floats from the French pontoon bridge were filled to excess with soldiers. Two sailors manned the vessels with soldiers on the oars. After a while, a blue flag with a white *A* appeared below the U.S. flag on the ships' masts, and each of the troops boats made for their brigade's tugboat, taking their place on the ropes. Here, the men dropped the oars and held on to the rope, twenty boats to a rope in some cases. After some jostling around and rearranging, the troops waited for the next maneuver.[163]

A shrill whistle from the tugboats blew, and the boats, with their charges trailing behind, began to churn through the grayish water. The boats began to pick up speed, heading to the ominously quiet shoreline. The usual chatter in the trailing craft ended, and every man looked fretfully ahead. Closing on the shoreline rapidly, the men were startled by two shrill whistles from the tugboats. Sailors in the rowboats yelled out in response, "Prepare to cast off!" Then, it happened: aboard the *Pilot Boy*, Foster spied a Confederate regiment and two guns near the Ashby house. Cries soon reverberated through the trailing boats that they were going to be under fire. Many bemoaned, and some started to loudly pray, but Foster ordered *Pilot Boy* to shear off its run at the Ashby beach and instead head half a mile northward to the Hayman house. Delayed while he waited for six lightweight naval howitzers to join his landing force, Reno was only ten minutes behind and compensated accordingly. The landing would be at Hayman's.[164]

At that moment, Lieutenant Stephen Quackenbush and the USS *Delaware* had been engaged in pounding Fort Bartow when a message ordered him to drift southward and aid the Union army's landing. Just as *Pilot Boy* prepared to make its run on the beach near Hayman's house, the *Delaware* arrived and began peppering the woods behind Hayman's soaked cornfields. *Picket* arrived, as per Foster's plan, at about the same time and added its guns to the barrage. An appreciative officer in the Tenth Connecticut wrote, "In the woods we could see the glitter of bayonets. A gunboat came up and sent a shell howling like a fiend through the woods." Across the fields, Colonel Jordan's Confederates melted away and marched back to the three-gun battery without attempting to dispute the Union landing.[165]

*Pilot Boy* chugged right into the mud flats, and soon, three quick, shrill whistles broke the air. Still some yards from the shoreline, the sailors in the rowboats yelled out, "Let go!" and the troops untied their little crafts and began make for the shore. The First Brigade was soon clambering ashore.[166]

Who was first on the island and with which flag became a contention among veterans of the landing, but one thing was for sure: the landing was anything but organized. Smith W. Higgins, one of the sailors in the first wave, ran ashore with a small flag from his vessel, the *Highlander*. Besides Higgins, Major Walter Bartholomew of the Twenty-seventh Massachusetts landed

Depicting the second assault wave, this image shows all the landing's elements: the tugboats dragging rowboats behind them, gunboats close to the shore providing covering fire and light draft transports landing the troops directly ashore. *From* Frank Leslie's Illustrated, *March 8, 1862.*

soon thereafter with the regimental colors. Nearby, Adjutant Harkness and Captain Richter of the Twenty-fifth Massachusetts stormed into Hayman's house and nailed a small flag outside the second-story window as a sign to the fleet. Inside the house, a telescope on the second floor pointing out to the fleet, a roaring fire in the kitchen and a table setting for an afternoon meal proved that the house had been hastily abandoned by a small Confederate outpost.[167]

In a short few minutes, 1,400 of Foster's men were landed, and while many of the men were too busy cheering themselves, two companies of the Tenth Connecticut did pass across the beachhead and set up a perimeter. They waded up to their waists through the creek at the eastern edge of Hayman's cornfield near the woods, spending three hours in water up to their knees. But they were alone. The bridgehead was, however, secure.[168]

As this was happening, *Patuxent* was arriving with Reno's men. As they hit the mud flats near the *Pilot Boy*, Reno didn't wait for the ships whistles but, with his stentorian voice, yelled out, "Let go!" The men stormed ashore with yells. The Twenty-first Massachusetts was sent to support the perimeter and relieved the two companies of the Tenth Connecticut, which, for the second time, waded through the chilly stream and returned to their regiment. The Fifty-first New York was sent to the north edge of Hayman's farm overlooking a marshy swamp, where it watched the end of the navy's bombardment of Fort Bartow two miles farther northward. The navy howitzers were split between the Twenty-first Massachusetts and the camp that Foster's men had begun to lay out.[169]

Parke came in a short time later on the *Phoenix*, parking in between Foster and Reno's landing areas. The right wing of the Fourth Rhode Island stormed ashore from the ship, while the Eighth Connecticut and Fifth Rhode Island waded in from the mud flats now at low tide and soon settled down for the night. After a quick conference, Foster, confident at the dispositions on the beachhead, left to start the second wave of landings, leaving Reno in charge.[170]

Back on the *Spaulding*, Burnside was all but teary at the success. "In less than twenty minutes from the time the boats reached the shore 4,000 of our men were passing over the marshes at a double quick and forming in most perfect order on dry land near the house," effused Burnside later. "I never witnessed a more beautiful sight." His men had successfully passed a huge hurdle in his campaign. This had never been accomplished in warfare before, and now his troops had landed without any resistance. After a quick on-scene inspection, Burnside found the generals had everything well in hand. The second wave was starting to offload, and the first wave was preparing for the oncoming night. It was the culmination of everything that had come before. The Coastal Division was a success, and so was Burnside.[171]

Back up the sound, the Confederate Navy saw the Union landing as well. Flag Officer Lynch decided to make another desperate run on the Union gunboats. If his ships could get in closer, they might be able to interfere with the landing. It was a desperate attack. Again, the *Sea Bird* led the Mosquito Fleet in its southward track. They passed the Confederate forts near the north end of the island and were cheered on by the waiting artillerymen. The ships approached the obstruction line, and just as before, disaster struck. This time, as the ships moved westward along the line, around 4:00 p.m., a plunging shot hit the *Curlew*, "as if she was made of paper." The ball went straight through, and the ship began to sink. In desperation, Captain Hunter drove the sinking ship toward the nearby shoreline, but the *Curlew* came to rest on a sandbar one hundred yards in front of Fort Forrest. The ship now stood blocking the fort's guns and could not be moved. All that could be done was for CSS *Fanny* to remove its remaining powder and shot and join the retreating fleet.[172]

Lynch's little navy had made two runs and lost two ships. All of the other ships had taken several hits, and many were no longer serviceable. With all of this, as well as being low on powder and shot, even after removing the *Curlew*'s supplies, Lynch made his decision. Realizing his fleet was of no further use, he abandoned Roanoke Island. He steamed off to Elizabeth City, across the Albemarle Sound, ostensibly for more ammunition, but when he towed off the *Black Warrior* behind his battered fleet, all knew he would not return. The Union navy was master of Croatan Sound.[173]

About nightfall, the second wave arrived ashore and completed many of the regiments that had landed incompletely on the first wave. General Parke returned to the island and moved into the Haymans' house, which had been allocated for headquarters. He, Reno and Parke spent most of the early part of the night going over the lay of the island with Robinson. Confederate forces were nearby but in what strength? The Twenty-first Massachusetts had already bumped into a Confederate patrol in the woods at the eastern end of the cornfield and lost one soldier. Reno's brigade was put on alert to cover the beachhead, with the Ninth New Jersey and Fifty-first Pennsylvania backing up the picketed troops. Foster's men were billeted around the house, while Parke's men occupied the southern end of the Hayman property.[174]

Each successive wave attempted to sort itself out and then find its respective brigades. By the time the third wave had arrived, just before 9:00 p.m., the shoreline had turned into a muddy slope, causing the arriving troops to slip and stumble in the mud or lose shoes in the darkness. In the Ninth New York, one of the last regiments landed that night, Sergeant John Whitney commented on the conditions, "The passage of so many regiments over the marsh had worked the soil into the consistency of soft clay." Pushing over a small stream that was drained by the falling tide, the Ninth New York was forced to cross on a small makeshift bridge of fence rails, the slickness of the ground forcing many men into the mud, with some astride the fence rails in painful positions. By 11:00 p.m., the landings were finally discontinued, with 11,500 men plus twelve pieces of artillery ensconced on the Hayman farm. Only one regiment had not been able to land, the Twenty-fourth Massachusetts, as its transport vessel, the *Guide*, had grounded within sight of the landing but could not free itself until later that night.[175]

Without cavalry, the generals and some staff officers had decided to ride down to the main road to investigate the area personally. At about 9:00 p.m., the impromptu reconnaissance passed the Twenty-first Massachusetts' picket line and moved to the main road. There, they viewed, in the faint light of an obscured half-moon, the ground for the next day's fight. In front of them, roughly half a mile ahead, lay the three-gun battery, and half a mile behind was the road to Ashby's where the Thirty-first North Carolina had been spied only hours before. To improve the defensive setup, the generals ordered Colonel Maggi to split his regiment in two wings with suitable artillery faced back to back to cover both roads in case the Confederates might have a force behind them as well as ahead. Then, the generals left the Massachusetts men to their dark, cheerless camp without any fires and commands in a barely audible whisper.[176]

The Union generals had good reason to realign their men. Less than 100 yards from the Massachusetts men holding the Hayman/Main Road intersection were Confederate skirmishers in a similarly cheerless skirmish line. The troops at the battery already stationed there, the Thirty-first and some companies of the Eighth North Carolina, were still filing in after marching up from the southern portion of the island at nightfall. As they milled about, Colonel Shaw arrived on the scene and began to parcel his forces. He ordered some of the companies of the Eighth to support Fort Bartow in case of a night landing there, while three companies were left at the battery, including Captain James Whitson. Whitson's men were placed in the woods to the right rear of the earthworks supporting the battery. Shaw ordered most of the Thirty-first North Carolina companies to march 250 yards farther behind the battery in the rear and deploy as a reserve force. Jordan, who claimed he had withdrawn from Ashby's in order to preserve the light artillery, left to command at Fort Bartow, leaving the reserves under Lieutenant Colonel Daniel Fowle. Fowle placed two companies of his unit, Captain Liles's Company B and Captain Charles Knight's Company F, in the entrenchments to either side of the battery. But the skirmishers were not from these regiments.[177]

After landing at Weir's Point that afternoon, the ten Confederate companies under Lieutenant Colonel Frank Anderson rushed down to reinforce the three-gun battery. Exhausted and blown by the time they arrived at the battery, Anderson's men were too spent to assault the beachhead. As the men filed into the woods to take what ease they could in the chilly night, Captain Obediah Wise approached Anderson with a request to take some twenty volunteers to locate and skirmish with the Union troops. Anderson, an antebellum filibuster soldier, saw the logic in this and, without consulting anyone else, gave Wise his approval. At about 7:00 p.m., Wise with ten men from his own "Norfolk Blues" company and ten men from the attached Louisianan "McCulloch Rangers" stalked through the brush. Two other volunteers, Thomas Dolan and Sumpter Williamson, soon joined Wise's push. Soon thereafter, Wise's men, still in the shadows of the woods, saw a Union skirmish line coming toward them. Each man took to a tree, and two shots opened on the Union skirmish line. Private Henry H. Howard fell screaming, shot through the hips, and the Massachusetts men abandoned the wood line to the Confederates.[178]

At about the time the generals returned to the Hayman house, the Twenty-first Massachusetts skirmish line returned to the realigned regimental position and the Ninth New York settled into its camp, the dread companion of the Union army in North Carolina—rain—made a reappearance.[179]

As per orders, the landing force had landed in "light marching order." No knapsacks, with change of clothes or sock or tents, were to be landed. The men carried blankets and rubberized ground covers. Wool overcoats did double duty battling the rain and the cold, while haversacks carried the remnant of three days' rations issued two days before. Only in cartridges were the men well prepared, carrying forty rounds each. The mud would dry off and the cold was defeated by fires, but the rain and wind seemed to cut through clothing; everyone remembered the night before the battle as a terrible event.

The rain that began about dark as a chilling mist built in intensity and, around 11:00 p.m., turned into a regular downpour. Few men could sleep in such weather. One man was Colonel Rush C. Hawkins of the Ninth New York. Having secured three fence rails that kept him out of the water, he wrapped up against the elements in a red wool blanket. As the wood became scarce, men started to look at Hawkins's bed for more firewood. Initially, men moved on when it was known that the sleeping figure was the colonel, but eventually, the call for more wood became a more important need than respect for the colonel. As Hawkins rolled on his side, two men stole the unused rail and ran into the night. Hawkins soon rolled off his plank bed and into the pooling water. Shocked, an understanding colonel simply readjusted his rails and went back to sleep, making sure he remained on his bed.[180]

Inside the Hayman house, a Ninth New York officer described the scene. The upstairs rooms were allocated to the officers and their staffs, while the downstairs areas were filled with officers trying to stay dry. "He was a lucky man who was able to get in that house," wrote the Zouave officer, "and luckier was he who could get a chair to sit in." Every bit of space was filled with officers. Lying down was a difficulty, as others searching for a place would trip on those secured. The Ninth officer found a place with an old friend who found an unused "room who had possession of a wood bench about two feet long, which he invited me to share with him." They spent the night on the bench, facing each other with their heads resting on each other's right shoulders. In the morning, they would be tired and achy but dry.[181]

Other officers were not as fortunate as Hawkins to have a bed or a bench. Captain Pardee of the Tenth Connecticut, reporting to headquarters at the Hayman house after his company's skirmish duty, found that the house was already filled, with officers lying on every square foot of the porch and house. Disgruntled, Pardee found a relatively dry spot underneath the porch on some cornstalks.[182]

Officers have special privileges, but the enlisted men stood outside in the elements. Soon they were surrounding their fence rail fires, attempting to keep warm and trying to dry most of the wet off their bodies. Some had food and cooked up, but mainly the men talked of home, family and what to expect in the battle the next day. All believed they would be heroes doing heroic deeds in that dark night. Dawn would tell.

# "We Are Going Under Fire Captain—Forward, Solidly, Quickly!"

Dawn arrived a little after 5:30 a.m. on February 8, but the sun, as on most winter days along the Outer Banks, was feebly trying to light the skies through a thick layer of fog. The musicians soon began playing their calls in the various camps. There was no attempt at stealth; the Confederates knew they were there anyway. In the upstairs rooms, Parke, Reno and Foster all went over the plan. Foster's First Brigade, with the naval howitzers in tow, would lead the way at 7:30 a.m. and march the one and a half miles to the Confederate battery. Reno would fall in and join the march, supporting Foster's four regiments with his four. Parke would dispatch two regiments to guard the landing and send two regiments forward if needed. Each commander handled his own brigade deployments. Although Foster was senior, there was no superior in command; each officer was to act as he saw fit.[183]

Below the officers' meeting rooms, the junior officers who had sought shelter from the storm were rudely awakened by Dr. Melancthon Storrs of the Eighth Connecticut Infantry as he and his attendants began to arrange the lower floor into operating rooms. Rousted from their poor sleep, the officers stumbled out to the commands, while the medical men relocated furniture or unhinged doors to use as tables to treat the expected wounded. Sheets, curtains and clothing were torn for bandages. While the tables were being set up and doctors laid out their instruments, others started to spread sand on the floors to soak up blood. Outside, the army stirred.[184]

Underneath the house, a fellow officer woke Captain Pardee of the Tenth Connecticut. In the half hour before the regiment marched, he polished off what was left of his rations, drank a cup of coffee and checked on his men. The lack of sleep had not affected him as he believed. Being in his first battle had, instead, revived him.[185]

At 7:00 a.m., Foster called his brigade to attention, and with the Twenty-fifth Massachusetts in the lead, they started down the cart path from the Hayman house toward the main road. Leading the Twenty-fifth Massachusetts, sour-looking Colonel Edwin Upton was happy and proud to be leading his regiment in this first attack. Behind the Twenty-fifth Massachusetts, the six twelve-pound Dahlgren naval howitzers on field carriages were dragged by a combined army/navy crew under Midshipman Benjamin Porter. Barely eighteen years old, Porter had bravery and intelligence in equal parts, and all his men were armed with cutlasses, pistols or rifles to defend their pieces if the unthinkable happened. The Twenty-third and Twenty-seventh Massachusetts Regiments followed the brass cannons. One of Parke's regiments, the Fifth Rhode Island, came next, if only to take over the southward-facing picket line from the Twenty-first Massachusetts as the column turned on to the main road. The Tenth Connecticut, the last of Foster's regiments on the island (the Twenty-fourth Massachusetts still hadn't landed), came up at the end of the column.[186]

Half a mile from the camp, the cart path crossed the tidal creek at a rocky ford. For some members of the Tenth Connecticut, this was the third time they were crossing the creek, and even at this planned crossing spot, the water was high. Many men remembered the water was cold and waist high, but they pushed on. As they marched, stray shots popped from the woods. Upton ordered Company A to shake out a skirmish line. Captain Josiah Pickett's men then moved northward into the woods. The fire increased for a time and then slackened as Upton's column continued its march.[187]

Captain Obediah Wise and his twenty-two men spent a nervous night in the woods. After their brush with the Twenty-first Massachusetts's Company G, they had settled into a rough skirmish line overlooking the Union campsite. Wise's men were shocked by how many fires there were, and a quick estimate proved beyond the shadow of a doubt that they were overwhelmingly outnumbered. At 7:00 a.m., they heard the Union army bands playing reveille and wondered when the fight would begin. They did not have to wait long. Looking across the swampy ground and into the cart path, they saw the long column start off. Wise had his men fire a few shots and then retreat slowly. As they started out, the Twenty-fifth Massachusetts's pickets rushed after them. Harried, Wise fell back about halfway to the three-gun battery where the rest of the McCulloch

Rangers, under Lieutenant Hazlett, came to his aid. From there, the skirmishers dueled along the main road in front of Foster's column.[188]

As Pickett's men scrimmaged with Wise and his troops, Foster passed the Twenty-first Massachusetts's six companies guarding the intersection. Maggi's men moved aside and cheered Foster's column as it turned left on to the main road. The Fifth Rhode Island then peeled off from the column and turned to the right, heading for Ashby's house about a mile southward. At the second intersection, the remaining companies of the Twenty-first Massachusetts were relieved and marched northward to reunite with the other companies. The Fifth Rhode Island soon took Captain Ashby's house without any resistance. A reunited Twenty-first Massachusetts at the northern intersection waited for Reno and the rest of its brigade. Ahead of it, Foster's column soon was out of sight. At about 8:30 a.m., there came a throaty "Huzzah!" and the sounds of cannon fire. The Battle of Roanoke Island had started.[189]

Pushing ahead of the column, Captain Pickett's skirmishers exited from the woods and found themselves on the edge of an open field. Seven hundred yards in front of them stood the Confederate battery with its three guns. Directly in front of them, Wise's little company fired sporadically and retired toward the entrenchments near the earthwork, splashing through the swampy ground as they went. Pickett advanced his men after the Confederates, and after about an hour of skirmishing in the swamp among the downed trees, he was relieved by the rest of the Twenty-fifth Massachusetts advancing up the main road. Colonel Upton ordered his column into line, and his men quickly went from column into a firing line stretching across the road. The ground on the right side was dry, and his right wing was quickly drawn up and firing at the Confederates, but the left wing, on the other side of the road, found the ground wet and filled with tall swamp grass entwined with tangle foot vines. The left wing was forced to hack its way through the grasses to establish its line, and one company commander believed that it "is only sending my men in there to be slaughtered." But soon the regiment was in line and volleying with the Confederates at the earthwork.[190]

Behind Upton, Porter's howitzers set up on the left side of the road. Upton, in order to give Porter some space to fire, ordered the Twenty-fifth Massachusetts to march to within three hundred yards of the earthwork and resume firing. It was begun in earnest, and the men cheered as they approached the Confederate works. The heavy humid air held the gunpowder smoke close to the ground, obscuring the soldiers' vision. "We could see nothing to shoot at, but taking our range by the smoke of the enemy's guns we blazed

Colonel Edwin Upton of the Twenty-fifth Massachusetts led his regiment in opening the Battle of Roanoke Island. *From Denny's* Wearing the Blue with the Twenty-fifth Massachusetts Volunteer Infantry, with Burnside's Coast Division, Eighteenth Army Corps and Army of the James.

away," wrote one Union soldier. "We fired high, low and obliquely, thinking if we covered a wide range of ground we might possibly lame somebody." The position change had not changed the conditions. The men were fighting in water in some places up to their knees, briars cut through their uniforms straight to their skins and officers found their swords worked best in cutting down the foliage. Back by the turn in the road, the howitzers began their salvos, sending shells over the fort.[191]

The officers led their men in different ways. Captain T.S. Foster of Company D was cutting briars with his sword, encouraging men, when he was hit near the right eye, which sent him spinning. Only the quick action of those near him saved the captain from drowning in the bog. Major Matthew McCafferty drew his pistol and, aiming it harmlessly into the sky, started firing. Still over three hundred yards away, his pistol was hopelessly out of range, and when asked what he was doing, McCafferty explained that at the high angle he was firing he estimated his shots would be raining down on the Confederates in an arcing path. Most of the men just chuckled. Colonel Upton cantered up and down his battle line, splashing water and mud, shouting encouragement to his men. The surgeon Dr. J. Marcus Rice set up a makeshift hospital behind the lines until he was wounded by a ball in his side.[192]

As the Twenty-fifth Massachusetts attempted to attack the fort by itself, General Foster ordered the recently drawn up Twenty-third and Twenty-seventh Massachusetts Regiments to move to the right and use the cover

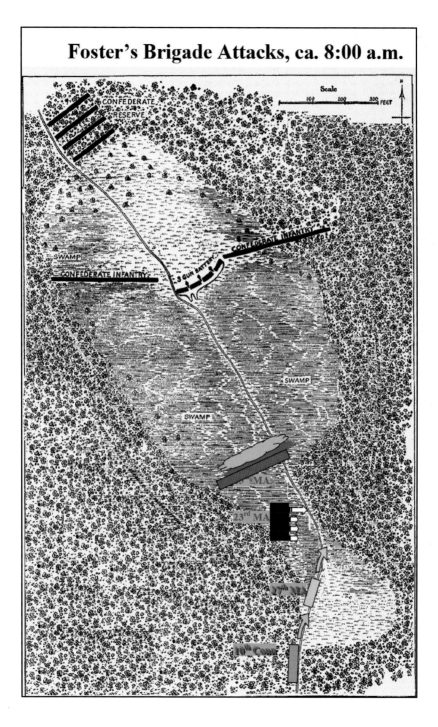

Foster's Brigade Attacks, ca. 8:00 a.m.

of a thick forest to mask their movements. But as the Twenty-fifth had already discovered, tracking in the island's swamps was a nightmare of bogs and entangling vines. The two regiments hacked their way toward the Confederate flank, but it was slow going. Regimental order broke down, with every company trying to cut its own path. Soon the Twenty-seventh lost contact with the Twenty-third, and then its companies became strung out in the swamp woods. Major Walter Bartholomew, angered by the glacial pace, went up the line and personally guided each company to the field's edge, fired a volley and then retired in the woods. This disjointed attack was essentially harmless but made Bartholomew feel like he was contributing. The Twenty-third, on the other hand, broke up into individual companies. Three of them continued northward and eventually did flank the Confederate entrenchments, but the remainder was as lost in the swamp as the Twenty-seventh. It would be hours before these regiments would influence the fight.[193]

After about an hour of fighting in the field, the Twenty-fifth Massachusetts was starting to run low on ammunition. Foster's aides brought up his reserve regiment, the Tenth Connecticut, and deployed them in line with Porter's gunners. Colonel Russell, on foot, ordered his men "forward, solidly and quickly." As the Twenty-fifth Massachusetts before it, the Tenth Connecticut discovered that the best ground was on the right of the road. Not having enough room for his entire regiment to form here, Russell put his men into two wings, one behind the other. They advanced forward twenty paces and halted. There, the first of many "friendly fire" incidents occurred as the Twenty-fifth Massachusetts started to file past the Tenth Connecticut's right flank. The Confederates, seeing the massed Union troops, opened on them with musket and artillery fire. The Tenth Connecticut's right wing cut loose in response to the Rebel fire before all of the Twenty-fifth Massachusetts companies had cleared the front. Three companies singed by the Union fire backtracked into the swamp and eventually passed the left flank of the Tenth, much perplexed at their situation. The reconstituted Twenty-fifth Massachusetts filed back to the edge of the open ground to await resupply. The time was about 9:00 a.m. The Twenty-fifth was not resupplied until late that afternoon, making it mere witness to the ever expanding battle.[194]

It was now the Tenth Connecticut's turn to try the Confederate defenses. Rifle fire burst on its massed ranks, plucking men from the ranks. Confederate snipers had also climbed the trees, hitting officers lying in the tall sawgrass. Russell's men soon received the Confederate artillerymen's attention. A shell burst in the front ranks, wounding four men. In Captain Pardee's company,

Lieutenant Stillman was pacing the rear when a ball hit him in the chest. Pardee ran to his aid only to hear him gasp and fall. Another soldier nearby was hit in his lower lip, causing a gruesome wound. Ordering the man to the rear to have it dressed, Pardee was surprised when he later found the same soldier trying to sneak back into the line. He had been to the surgeon but hadn't had his fill of fighting yet.

Mercifully, Russell gave the orders for his men to lie down, dodging most of the Confederate fire. While the Tenth soldiers were lying down, Colonel Charles Russell stood for every man to see. Constantly viewing the field with binoculars, Russell was reproached by his men. While shunning their concerns, Russell was greeted by a singular incident. Lieutenant Colonel de Monteil, formerly of the Fifty-third New York, approached the standing colonel carrying a German target rifle. De Monteil, still trying to prove his competency and bravery, was now fighting as a private soldier. Carrying the heavy target rifle, de Monteil was looking for a spotter to see the effects of his high-powered rifle on the Confederates. Russell consented, and for a few shots, Russell viewed the Frenchman's accuracy, telling him how to readjust; all the while, Confederate bullets spat at the dust around them. This little marksmanship lesson was interrupted by the Tenth's lieutenant colonel, Albert Drake, who chased off the Frenchmen, suggesting he find some woods to hide in and stop attracting attention. A perplexed Russell pardoned Drake's actions, but de Monteil took the suggestion and moved on.

Drake also convinced Russell to seek cover. While behind Company H, the men pleaded with their colonel. "Colonel that one was meant for you—lie down—do lie down," they often repeated. Finally he relented, and as he did, a bullet smacked into his shoulder, hitting his heart as it passed through his body. Russell was dead instantly. The Tenth Connecticut was frozen with inactivity. Foster's brigade was played out, with two regiments bogged down in the swamps, one out of ammunition and the last one pinned down. It was barely 9:30 a.m., and the Union forces were stalled.[195]

# "It Was the Hardest Place I Ever Saw"

Colonel Alberto Maggi was impatiently waiting for the rest of the brigade at the crossroads. His regiment was reunited now, and he panted for the fight, which he could plainly hear just up the road. General Reno could not get there fast enough, and as soon as he saw Reno's troops marching up the road from the Hayman house, Maggi ordered his men into column on the road, ahead of the other column instead of behind. Reno, appreciating the Italian's fervor, did not chide or correct him but silently gave Maggi the order to lead the column. It didn't take the Second Brigade long to come up on the rear of Foster's brigade.[196]

"We went a half mile through three feet of water, and saw them bring the wounded out of the swamp. I saw one who was shot through the stomach by a cannon ball, and many who were shot in the arm or leg," wrote Private Charles Miller. With the limited amount of space, the columns were narrowed to two men wide, giving way to the wounded from the Twenty-fifth Massachusetts. Wounded men cheered on the new arrivals with cries of "We're driving them," or "Just go on up and finish what we started." All the green soldiers could see, however, were the wounds, the blood and gore.[197]

Arriving on the battlefield at about 9:30 a.m., Reno quickly conferred with Foster, who had taken his post by Porter's cannons. It was immediately obvious that the path to the right was already clogged with troops, and the Tenth Connecticut, which was still filing into position near the cannons, was pinned down. Left was the only direction remaining. Reno ordered Maggi and his Bay Staters to push into the swampy forest on the left of the road

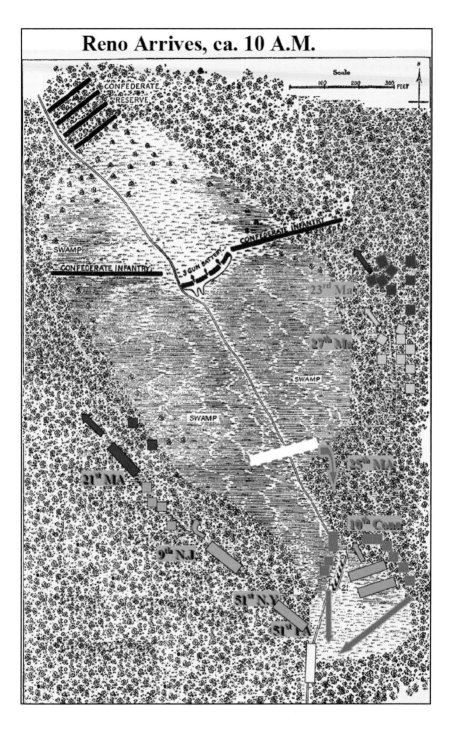

Reno Arrives, ca. 10 A.M.

and try to flank the fort's defenders. Quickly obeying, Maggi ordered his men into the morass.[198]

Like the other side of the road, the forest was overgrown with tangle foot vines and boggy terrain. Private Miller commentated that "it was the hardest place I ever saw—nothing but cane and thorns, thick as rye," which tore at their clothing and cut their hands and faces. The swampy conditions made organized marching nearly impossible. Maggi sent his two skirmish companies, D and G, forward to drive off any Rebel outposts, but they made little progress ahead of the column. The Twenty-first Massachusetts struggled in the swamp, peppered the entire time by the Confederate defenders at the three-gun battery.[199]

Behind Maggi came Ferrero's Fifty-first New York, and Reno sent them after the Massachusetts regiment. They too soon became bogged down in the knee-deep mud of the island's swamps, and like the regiments on the other side of the road, the Fifty-first New York became scattered. The road march paced slowed and soon took on the pace of a funeral procession as the New Yorkers crept forward. Then, with a cheer, the Ninth New Jersey, under orders from Foster and Reno, rushed up the trampled pathway, breaking through the New Yorkers' line. In an effort to aid Porter's gunners and the Tenth Connecticut, Reno ordered Lieutenant Colonel Charles Heckman's New Jerseymen forward to find a suitable place to fire on the battery. Heckman's twelve companies strung out on the line would produce a lot of firepower, but Heckman, excited to prove his worth, rushed forward energetically. Still saddened by the loss of their beloved colonel and surgeon, the regiment looked for revenge. His men overran the main body of Ferrero's New Yorkers and had only advanced less than two hundred yards when Heckman ordered his companies to wheel to the right and form a column of divisions. With this, the two companies formed a battle line and advanced to the edge of the field. Behind them, the other ten companies formed five more battle lines and squatted down in the water to await their turn to fight. Heckman personally led his first division out and commenced firing on the Rebels. As the divisions neared the bottom of their cartridge boxes, Heckman rotated them with the next division, peeling away to the rear, allowing the next division to advance and fire. This revolving fire kept up a good rate of fire and kept the men together. For Heckman, the battle was here. He would not even try to take his men farther on. A sensible commander who knew his and his men's limitations, Heckman would not be moved.

But behind him, the improvised roadway that the Twenty-first had hacked through the swamp was not possible for his successive lines. Ferrero was forced

Lieutenant Colonel Charles Heckman commanded the Ninth New Jersey. *From Drake's History of the Ninth New Jersey Veteran Volunteers.*

to hack a new trail around the New Jersey regiment, creating an ever-increasing gap between his main body and the four companies that had followed the Massachusetts troops toward the Confederate right.

Ferrero's wayward companies were in good hands. Lieutenant Colonel Robert Potter had advanced the first three companies in a hurry to keep tabs on Maggi's men. When the Twenty-first Massachusetts's pace became slowed when it hit an exceptionally wet portion of the woods, Potter discovered that he had become separated from the main body of the Fifty-first. Potter could have sat and waited for Ferrero but decided to join Maggi's column. Potter was later joined by the color company, which just followed the trampled path the column had created, making his detachment four companies strong. As the column advanced in the woods, Confederate artillery rounds boomed in protest after them, bouncing among the trees.[200]

Soon Reno's last regiment, the Fifty-first Pennsylvania, struggled up the road. The procession was slow and arduous. For much of it, the Fifty-first Pennsylvania remained at rest, waiting for the path to clear. Nearby the surgeons had established a triage center where the dead and dying were separated from the wounded who would be sent back to the Hayman house. Casualties came by with all manner of wounds, and the soldiers could only stand by and watch as men were operated on beside them in the road. Colonel Hartranft, looking to get his men into the action, soon had the Pennsylvanians marching up the trampled path on the left and was not far on the path when his lead companies bumped into Heckman's rear companies.

Conferring with Heckman and hearing that the Fifty-first New York was bogged down farther up the road, Hartranft ordered his men to about face. Leaving two companies in the pathway to aid the others in any manner, he took the rest of the regiment across the road behind Porter's gunners and collided with the woods on the right. In his haste to enter the battle and redeem his honor, Hartranft had not searched out the path cut by the Twenty-third and Twenty-seventh Massachusetts Regiments but was cutting a new path through the swampy grounds. This breaking new ground tied up the regiment for the rest of the day, and as such, the Pennsylvanians lost only one wounded that day.[201]

Hearing little fire from his brigade, Reno and his staff splashed up the path searching for his regiments. The logjam stymied the Pennsylvanians, and Reno needed to find out personally why his men were stalled. On foot, Reno soon found Heckman and New Jerseymen pounding volleys across the swamp. Heckman's report confirmed Reno's fear of the terrain, and he applauded Heckman on deployment. Running farther up the path, he found Ferrero's men sitting in the mud. Passing the New Yorkers, Reno just ordered Ferrero to do his best to get into the fight. Reno headed on, wondering where Maggi was. He soon found him; two companies of the Twenty-first Massachusetts were skirmishing with the Confederates around the three-gun battery. The rest of the regiment filed past and began deploying into line in a cleared swampy area to the west. Trailing behind his column, Potter and his four wayward companies followed behind.

Reno saw what Maggi had accomplished and ordered the Twenty-first Massachusetts to charge. The New England soldiers gave out a loud, wild yell and rushed into the swamp. Beside them, Potter's New Yorkers broke out of the woods, which were so thick it was almost impossible to see out of them; both units rushed forward. Then, the Confederates hit them with a salvo from two of their cannons and musketry. The combination of the swampy water, up to the men's waist in some circumstances, and the volley stopped Maggi's attack cold. His men began to return fire. Reno tried to restart the charge, but it would take time. The men—hungry, tired and freezing cold in the swampy water—were reacting slowly. Reno was concerned the men were effectively pinned down as they were, and there was no telling if there were Confederates in the woods to the north. If there were, Maggi's men could in turn be flanked by Confederate reserves. He needed his men to move.[202]

It was a little after 11:00 a.m., and fewer than one thousand Confederates and their nightmarish terrain had stalled the attack of nearly eight thousand Union troops. Foster's men were still struggling to find a path to the Confederates on the Union right flank, while Reno's men had become bogged down on the Union left. Foster ordered Parke's troops up. Maybe the infusion of fresh troops would tip the balance.

John Parke's role in the battle plan was to guard the beachhead. To this end, the Fifth Rhode Island had been sent to relieve the Twenty-first Massachusetts when Foster's brigade moved out at 7:00 a.m. Therefore, when the call came from the front for Parke to come up, he wasn't prepared.

The Fifth Rhode Island had arrived at the Ashby house at about the time Foster's regiments were attacking the three-gun battery. Rushing the house, the understrength Rhode Island regiment easily captured the five-man outpost, but this represented a quandary. Outposts are usually the lead element of larger units—was there still one in the area, behind the Union front lines? There had been one Confederate regiment on the farmstead the day before when the Union troops first landed, but it had melted into the woods soon thereafter. The captured soldiers, of course, were no help. They told outlandish

stories of thousands of Confederates waiting in the swamps to set upon the Union attacks. Major John Wright decided to play a trick of his own. Taking the captured soldiers to a spot on the Ashby farm where the men could see the Union army gearing for battle, Wright told

Major John Wright of the Fifth Rhode Island, seen here in later years, was sent to occupy the Ashby house area. *From Burlingame's* History of the Fifth Rhode Island, *1892.*

them they were paroled and could return to their regiment, knowing full well that they would tell their comrades what they had seen. He hoped that the vast army arrayed about the Hayman house would convince these men of the overwhelming numbers. Wright's plan, though convincing enough, was unnecessary, as the outpost had been left behind when Jordan's Thirty-first North Carolina left the area the night before. Still, Parke had to be aware that the beachhead could be in danger.[203]

Parke's other regiments, the Eighth Connecticut, Fourth Rhode Island and Hawkins's Ninth New York Zouaves guarded the beachhead. They could only stand and listen with jealous interest as the cannons boomed and musketry sounded as if tearing sheets. They occasionally heard the cheers from one thousand throats. Then, they also saw the battle's casualties as they were carried from the battlefield to the Hayman house. Dr. Storrs, aided by other regimental surgeons, was soon inundated with casualties. Needing space, Storrs ordered Assistant Surgeon Potter and Surgeon Minnis of the Ninth New Jersey to expand the surgery by commandeering the Ashby house. A small bridge was constructed over the dividing creek connecting the two farms. The screams and incessant sawing unnerved the new troops.

After the Twenty-fifth Massachusetts's surgeon J. Marcus Rice was wounded, a triage center was set up two hundred yards behind the naval howitzers. There, Brigade Surgeon Thompson quietly attended the wounded with aid from bandsmen. As there were no wagons or horses, the men were carried back by stretcher or pushcart. Many of those who

Among the numerous physicians trying to aid the wounded on the Union side was Assistant Surgeon Albert Potter of the Fifth Rhode Island. *From Burlingame's* History of the Fifth Rhode Island, *1892.*

were minorly wounded and still ambulatory were pointed in the direction they needed to go and sent on their way. It was gruesome.[204]

As the morning faded, the procession of casualties steadily increased, and so did the cries for water and cartridges. Already the Twenty-fifth Massachusetts had used up its supply of ammunition. It did what it could, but without cartridges, all it could really provide was moral support for the attacking troops. Other regiments, such as the Tenth Connecticut and Ninth New Jersey, were dueling with the Confederates and would soon be running low as well. What would happen then?

The answer came at about this time in the form of the much-delayed Twenty-fourth Massachusetts Infantry. While the rest of the army was ashore in its cold bivouac, the Twenty-fourth remained stuck on a sandbar. Its ship, the *Guide*, had run aground and remained so until well into the night. Now, as the morning haze burned off and the Union navy started its bombardment again, the steamer *Guide* came into Ashby's Harbor not only with the fresh regiment but also with several thousand rounds of ammunition. Quickly offloaded, three companies of the Twenty-fourth Massachusetts were ordered to remain, offload the ammunition and carry it up to the battle lines.[205]

Now, with the Twenty-fourth Massachusetts and the ammunition, Parke felt secure enough to send his two regiments forward as per Foster's orders. At about 11:00 a.m., the Fourth Rhode Island and Ninth New York marched down the cart path as all the other regiments had done that morning. Behind them seven companies of the Twenty-fourth, carrying as many crates of ammunition as they could, followed. The battle was about to hit its climax.[206]

# "This Fire Is Very Hot"

It might have seemed from the Union side that the Confederates were holding off their attacks with ease, but it was merely a façade. Amateur officers Shaw and Jordan, knowing they were out of their element, left the Confederate defensive plans to Lieutenant Colonel Frank Anderson of the Fifty-ninth Virginia, who had all that he could handle. The old filibuster, who had fought in Nicaragua in the 1850s, fed the troops into the battle and rotated exhausted units with such precision the Union troops thought they were fighting a much larger force.[207]

It began with Wise's detachment. By 8:30 a.m., the Union troops had pushed Wise's skirmishers back to the southern edge of the field. There, Wise and Lieutenant Hazlett fell back to the entrenchments, with Wise's Norfolk Blues falling back on to the Confederate left and Hazlett's Rangers on the right. They continued to pepper the Union regiments as they pushed through the boggy wooded swamps. The earthworks soon received the focus of the Union attacks.[208]

Inside the three-gun battery, the guns were arrayed, with Lieutenant William Selden volunteering to command the little six-pounder on the center embrasure, fronting on the road. Still smarting from some comments by General Wise as to his engineering talents, Selden hoped his combat prowess would vindicate him. On either side were the other guns. To Selden's left, Captain Schermerhorn and crew served the eighteen-pounder trophy cannon, facing the Union right. On Selden's right, Lieutenant T.C. Kinney commanded the twenty-four-pound howitzer, aiming on the woods of the Union left flank. The guns were effectively sited but were limited in ammunition. There was ample shot and shell for the six-pounder, but the eighteen-pounder was limited in solid shot while both larger guns had to make due with twelve-pound canister rounds. The earthwork was arranged in a semicircle, its walls four feet high with embrasures. An eight-foot-wide and three-foot-deep moat impeded direct attack. Gunners and cannons were crammed into the thirty-five-foot-wide entrenchment, and the trenches for the supporting infantry could only field a further two hundred men, forcing most of Anderson's men into supporting roles.[209]

When the battle began, Captain James Whitson's Company B, Eighth North Carolina, and two companies from the Thirty-first North Carolina were crammed in the trenches. Rifles were fired so quickly as to become too hot to hold. Cannons belched forth with canister, slowing Union attacks. To further boost Wise's company, Anderson dispatched Captain Robert Coles's company, also from the Forty-sixth Virginia, and they kept the Twenty-third Massachusetts's advance to a crawl.[210]

After nearly an hour and a half of intense fighting at the three-gun battery, Anderson began to see the North Carolinians waiver. Many were running low on ammunition and were still tired from their all-day marching the day before. Anderson rotated the three companies with three from the reserve—Companies E and K of the Fifty-ninth Virginia and Captain Edward Yellowley's Company G from the Eighth North Carolina—and continued the fight. The troops' switch did attract attention from the Union artillery, and four men were wounded in the exchange, but otherwise the rotation was effected without a misstep.[211]

All throughout the day, the artillery kept pounding the Union attackers, sending loads of canister and shell into the woods. But the Union rifles were quick to return the favor. In the trenches near the guns, Second Lieutenant N.G. Munro of the Eighth North Carolina was stalking behind his men, keeping their spirits up when a rifle round hit him in the head, killing him instantly. The trenches were not as safe as they should have been with Union troops closing on three sides.[212]

Behind the earthworks, the Confederate casualties were piling up and were being attended by valiant Confederate surgeons like Dr. Sandy Gordon. Gordon, who had just been assigned to the Wise Legion, had spent the morning preparing a farmyard along Shallowbag Bay, about a mile and a half the battlefield as the Confederate hospital, but when overshooting Union gunboats started to drop rounds about the farm, Gordon felt he would venture closer to the front and take his chances. Coming up to the reserve line, Gordon's ducking and running caught Lieutenant Colonel Anderson's eye. He called out to the crouching doctor, "Doctor, you can walk faster and lower to the ground than any man I ever saw." In this moment of fear and panic, the laughter was needed to break the tension.

Gordon soon set up as close to the front line as he could and set up a triage center, sending even the dead to the hospital so he didn't frighten the new troops. He would have a lot work before the day was over.[213]

More Confederate troops were on the way to join the fight for Roanoke Island. General Wise, still trying to fight the battle from his sickbed, ordered Major Henry Fry of the Forty-sixth Virginia to ferry over five companies of the Forty-sixth Virginia, about 150 men, to the island to reinforce Anderson at the three-gun battery. Taking the same tender and boats that had conveyed Anderson the morning before, Fry's men set a course directly for Roanoke Island instead of landing at Weir's Point, which was once again under fire. Fry commenced landing at about 10:00 a.m., but it would be some time before they arrived at the battery.[214]

At about this time, Wise's expected reinforcements from Wilmington, Colonel J. Wharton Green's Second North Carolina Battalion, were arriving on the island after a harrowing venture. The weeklong railroad trip was not half as frightening as the last twelve hours aboard ships had been. Leaving Elizabeth City on the seventh, Green's little convoy steamed through the night to make the island. At 2:00 a.m. on the eighth, the tender, with seven transports in tow, had come to anchor in the middle of the Albemarle Sound to wait for morning. Green's pilot had become lost in the darkness and would not move on until he could get his bearings. Suddenly from out of the inky blackness, several shapes were seen coming toward them. At first it as thought that they were Union gunboats from Roanoke Island, but soon it was discovered they were Lynch's Mosquito Fleet running back to Elizabeth City for ammunition and repairs. The darkened ships, however, just steamed past, making no signals, and one of the steamers, the *Beaufort*, collided with one of Green's transports. As soon as the Mosquito Fleet had arrived, they were gone as fast as their wood burning engines could carry them. Fortunately, the transport remained afloat, and by 10:00 a.m., Green's ships began to offload their men and cargo on the north end of Roanoke Island, where Anderson's men had come ashore the day before. It would be nearly two hours before Green's men would be fully assembled. It was just a matter of time if Fry and Green's men would make a difference in the battle.[215]

At the forts, the Union gunboats resumed their bombardment as soon as the fog burned off, but with the infantry engaged, the navy did not see a need to be as fully engaged as they had the day before. A worry of naval shells overshooting and hitting the advancing infantry was a constant fear; therefore, navy gunners withdrew to the limits of their rifled cannons and sent high arching shells into Fort Bartow. The fort, which had been repaired by slave laborers the night before, responded as it had the day before with a few spattered rounds to convince the navy that the fort was still manned. The U.S. Navy would fire fewer than one hundred rounds this day, as opposed to nearly six hundred it fired in the earth-shattering bombardment the day before. On the mainland, Fort Forrest was still screened by the wreckage of the CSS *Curlew*. The sound was unusually peaceful as compared to the island.[216]

The pressure continued to build all across the Confederate front. In the late morning, on the right flank, as Hazlett's company was driven back to the shelter of the three-gun battery by the Twenty-first Massachusetts, the Union rifle shots were taking effect in the battery. Anderson ordered Captain Whitson's company back into action. With some Roanoke Island natives in his company, Anderson hoped that Whitson's company knew of some pathway to flank the Union attack force. With ten men in advance, Whitson's company attempted to feel its way through the brush, hoping to catch the Federals from behind. As Hazlett fell back, the Confederate left flank was also coming under heavy fire.[217]

In the dense undergrowth of the swampy woods, companies of the Twenty-third Massachusetts ran into Coles's and Wise's companies. The intense firefight attracted more and more of the disjointed Massachusetts companies that were lost in the swamp. Soon a full-fledged battle was being waged among the cypress, pines and sawgrass. Captain Coles, son of a Philadelphia merchant, found himself next to Captain Wise in the woods. Wise, turning to Coles, yelled over the din, "This fire is very hot; tell Colonel Anderson we must fall back or be reinforced." Coles nodded in agreement and, as he turned to leave, was shot and instantly killed. The Confederates were reaching their breaking point.[218]

12

# "Where Duty Calls Me"

At about 11:30 a.m., Parke's two regiments started to file onto the battlefield. What they saw was fearful. The dead and dying were lying all around. Porter's howitzers were standing idle, unmanned, with the exception of Porter and the Twenty-fifth Massachusetts's chaplain, Horace James. The battery's ammunition was too low to continue to duel with

Naval Lieutenant Porter kept up an effective bombardment with his naval howitzers until ammunition ran short. *From Abbott's* Heroic Deeds of Heroic Men.

the Confederates. The Tenth Connecticut was nearby, lying unseen in the sawgrass. The rest of the area was a seething, smoky cauldron. "The dense wood and heavy atmosphere held the powder smoke like a pall over the battery," wrote one Tenth Connecticut private. Troops in the rear area were exhausted and powder stained. A newspaper correspondent was behind a tree making notes, carefully peeking around the tree between volleys and then back to his notes.[219]

Soon up came General Parke, almost laughing, shouting, "That's right! Come on! We have plenty of men; more than we know what to do with—the day will be ours!" His comment could not have been truer. On the Union right, the Twenty-third Massachusetts was battling Wise's skirmishers, while the Twenty-seventh Massachusetts was volleying with the three-gun battery from the cover of the woods. The Tenth Connecticut was pinned down, not risking raising their heads above the grass. The Twenty-fifth Massachusetts was waiting for ammunition but was effectively out of the battle. The Ninth New Jersey was fighting from the swamps, and the Twenty-first Massachusetts and part of the Fifty-first New York were trying to fight back from the swampy ground on the Union left. The rest of the Fifty-first New York and all of the Fifty-first Pennsylvania were just trying to find a place to fight from. The scene was confusion.[220]

Parke soon started the Fourth Rhode Island down the first path he came to on the right side of the road. Unfortunately, that was being hacked out of the swamps by the Fifty-first Pennsylvania, and it had not progressed very far. The Ninth New York was ordered to follow the Fourth, but the going was slow. Like those before, the Ninth New York viewed the casualties as they filed off the field. Swedish-born private Charles Johnson wrote, "Many others passed us in ghastly array: a Captain, assisted by a couple of men, had apparently an eye torn out; another, in a sitting position, was spewing pure blood; but none seemed to freeze my very life as that terrible spectacle of the spasmodic stump with its severed arteries squirting blood."

In the center of the Zouaves stood their colors, carried by the biggest and strongest soldiers in the regiment. Besides the Stars and Stripes and the Ninth's large, red silk color was Corporal John William Pattison, an iron molder from Peekskill, New York. Pattison had just refused a promotion and orders to rejoin his company in order to be with the colors and, with patriotic fervor, had cushioned the blow in a letter to his parents, "I must go where duty calls me, if it is to the cannon's mouth that duty I would not refuse to do." Pattison looked over the field at "the greatest sight I ever saw." "There lay our troops in the swamps and behind trees up to their

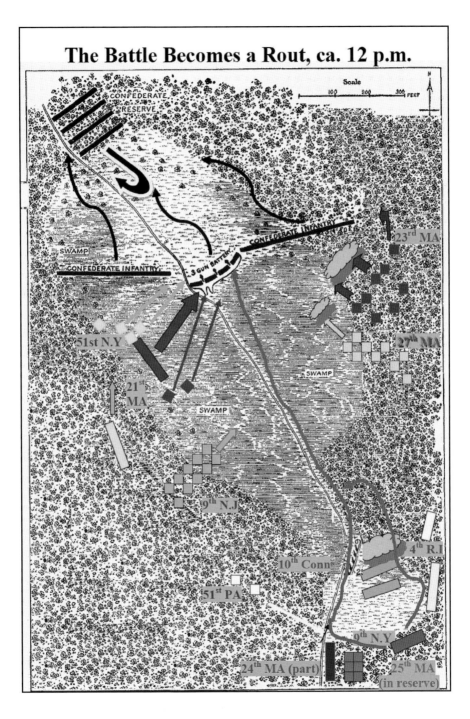

The Battle Becomes a Rout, ca. 12 p.m.

An ironworker from Peekskill, New York, Color Corporal John William Pattison would describe the battle in a letter to his parents. *From the Peekskill Museum in Peekskill, New York.*

waists in water. They was getting shot faster than the men with stretches could carry them off," he wrote home later.[221]

As the red-fezzed Ninth New York joined the march across the field, the Confederates sent the men a warm reception. Rifle bullets sang over their heads. Johnson and others around were suddenly consumed by the "sickening sensation as if I was going to a slaughter house to be butchered." Everything was confusion. As they neared the bend in the road where Porter's guns were located, a naval gun crew, spying the Confederates about to fire, informed the Ninth New York that it was targeted. With a cry, the colorful Zouaves dropped onto their stomachs as a wave of canister passed over their heads. Although the Zouaves had been under fire before, they had never been in an engagement this large. Some of the men suddenly broke and ran for the rear. They didn't get far. The Fifty-first Pennsylvania's two companies remaining on the left of the road and the lead companies of Twenty-fifth Massachusetts stood in their path with fixed bayonets and ordered the stragglers back with cries of, "No Bull Runs here." The would-be deserters meekly rejoined the regiment and the chaos.[222]

Other men, individually and in company strength, sought to relieve the tension by firing on the Confederates; unfortunately, they were not briefed on where the Union troops were. Charles Johnson and others settled to the right of the road and took aim. While Johnson misfired, many other Zouaves fired, accidentally hitting the Ninth New Jersey. It took some time to calm down the high-energy and nervous Zouaves.[223]

Farther ahead, at the head of the Ninth's column, Colonel Hawkins was greeted by "volunteer" de Monteil. After being chased off from the Tenth Connecticut, de Monteil had wandered the battlefield trying to find a place to set up his heavy target rifle. Seeing the Zouaves, the old French officer joined them, marching into the woods. The old lieutenant colonel kept calling the Zouaves *mes enfants*, French for "my children." The New Yorkers thought nothing of the old man.[224]

Foster and Parke were looking at the Confederate lines for any weaknesses. Through their binoculars, the smoke-shrouded battery still retained its strength. At that point, a Confederate officer stood on the breastworks to cheers of his soldiers. The brave officer dared Union rifle fire, which soon obliged, and he tumbled off the parapet. The troops who were cheering a moment before could be seen leaving the works in small groups. Was this the moment? Did the Confederates reach the breaking point? Now was the time to charge.[225]

At that moment, Parke felt a tug at his sleeve and saw Major Edgar Kimball, Hawkins's third in command, standing in a

Fiery and quick to anger, few could call Lieutenant Colonel Edgar Kimball cowardly. He led his section of the Ninth New York forward at Roanoke Island. *From the Library of Congress.*

salute among the flying bullets. Kimball, a tall, bewhiskered Mexican War veteran, gruffly requested to charge the battery. Parke and Foster nodded in agreement, and Foster gave Kimball his orders in true dramatic fashion, "Now is the time, and you are the men; charge the battery!"[226]

With a flourish, Kimball drew his sword and ordered the Ninth New York to follow him. With the left wing of the regiment, Kimball retraced his steps through the woods, across the field and onto the main road, all the time the Zouaves chanting their French battle cry, "Zou, zou, zou!" Back at the head of the column, Hawkins, who had not been informed of the command, saw half his regiment suddenly turn around and start for the road. With the men left, Hawkins ordered his chief bugler, Thomas Flockton, to blow the charge. "And away went the boys with a yell up to their waists in water," remembered Pattison. The bugle sounded clear and resonated across the

Hawkins's Zouave bugler Thomas Flockton; his bugle blast sounded the final portion of the battle. *From Naylor's* Civil War Days in a Country Village.

field. Everyone knew that the moment of decision was at hand.[227]

When Flockton blew his bugle, the Union troops were themselves in a critical position. The Twenty-third Massachusetts had driven Wise's skirmishers back to the entrenchments, and four Union companies had already pushed beyond the Rebel left flank and were firing on the Confederate reserve. The rest of the Twenty-third's companies were firing on the eastern face of the three-gun battery, pinning down Captain Schermerhorn's gun crew. The Twenty-seventh Massachusetts was doing something similar farther southward, as that regiment's main body had advanced to the edge of the field and fired on the earthwork. Major Bartholomew was planning to push his men into a full charge on the earthwork at the time, but some wild volleys from the Tenth Connecticut forced him to reconsider, and the Twenty-seventh Massachusetts soon retreated back into the woods, seeking relief from the scorching friendly fire.[228]

On the other side of the road, the Ninth New Jersey had already rotated through half of its divisions, meaning most of the New Jersey regiment had already fired off their forty rounds of ammunition. If the battle continued much longer, Colonel Heckman would have to withdraw. Under the immense smoke clouds from the volleys, Heckman could see little of the battle. He ordered some of the regiment's best shots into the trees to have something to fire at. Their vision above the regiment wasn't much better. The only time the smoke cleared for a moment was when the cannons let loose with a round. The compact New Jersey regiment was a tempting target, and one round hit with incredible effectiveness. One of the six-pound rounds came

An example of the terrain the right flank of the Union attack had to contend with is shown in this *Battle and Leaders* sketch. *From Johnson and Buell's* Battles and Leaders of the Civil War, *volume 1.*

zipping through the smoke and tall grass, carrying away both of Corporal John Lorence's legs; then it took off Private Jonathan Bural's right leg and passed through Private Isaac V.D. Blackwell, killing him instantly, before it smashed into Captain Joseph J. Henry's chest, crushing him. Heckman's volleys were tearing into the Confederates and quite possibly Maggi and his men as well. Then, at around 11:00 p.m., a cry of "There they go!" was heard from Lieutenant Samuel Hufty, who had climbed up into the trees with the marksmen. With that, Heckman ordered his men to advance into the fields. There they received two volleys from their right rear. One might have come from the Ninth New York, which was now in full charge, but the other might have come from the Tenth Connecticut, which had been firing in that direction. Unaware of the Ninth New Jersey's advance, the Connecticut men did not hold their fire, causing a few casualties and no small amount consternation among the New Jersey troops.[229]

When Flockton blew his bugle, the Twenty-first Massachusetts and four companies of the Fifty-first New York were trying to sort themselves out and return fire on the Confederates at the earthworks. Potter's New Yorkers had also tangled with some Confederates in the brush to their north, insinuating a possible Confederate flank attack. Maggi had his men lie down to withstand the Confederate fire. Charles Miller remembered, "This volley checked us, and we commenced firing without order, but we were ordered to cease firing and lay down, and so they all did, but me."

Frazar Stearns, adjutant of the Twenty-first Massachusetts, the only son of the president of Amherst College and a close friend of poetess Emily Dickinson, learned the harsh realities of war at Roanoke Island. *From* Adjutant Stearns, *1862.*

Miller, standing in water up to his thighs, decided to stand instead and testified to heavy Rebel fire: "It mowed the bushes down before us; it cut the cap-box off of my belt; one ball went through my cartridge-box, and three through my clothes, but none touched me."[230]

It wasn't just the private soldiers who experienced this heavy fire. Adjutant Frazar Stearns, son of the Amherst College president, was roaming behind the lines, yelling encouragement to the riflemen near Colonel Maggi and General Reno, when a buckshot pellet smashed into his forehead, sending the young lieutenant to the ground. Stunned and bleeding profusely, Stearns had the foresight to tie a handkerchief around his head to stem the wound. He got groggily to his feet, turned to Captain Charles Walcott and joked, "A man never gets hit twice in the same fight—does he captain?" No sooner had those words been said than another round creased Stearns's neck, creating an ugly flesh wound that just missed his spine. As if the Confederate fire wasn't bad enough, while it tried to rally for the charge, the Twenty-first took a few volleys and stray artillery rounds from its blue comrades. The charge had to be made.[231]

General Reno saw the situation and knew the Twenty-first had to charge. Running up to Maggi, Reno shouted over the din, "Colonel Maggi, can you charge and take that battery?" A confident Maggi yelled back, "We can, General!" With that, Maggi and his men stood up and, with bayonets fixed, charged across one hundred yards of cleared swampy ground. A Fifty-first New York soldier writing to his hometown paper remembered:

> *There was no time to be lost, and the enemy's fire was thinning our ranks rapidly; one poor fellow at my side looking me in the face cried: "My God, I have got two bullets at once," and he fell at my feet.—"Forward!" says the Captain; and I had no chance to help him. But the enemy is before us; we see the rebels face to face; "Charge," is the order, and with one shout of triumph, and one rush upon them they flew back, and in a few seconds we were in the Fort.*

Maggi's little force rushed over some difficult terrain, and the men were confused, attacking in small groups here and there. Corporal Ethan Blodgett, carrying the white Massachusetts state flag, led the first group over the Confederate entrenchments and right embrasure of the battery. The honor of the first national flag on the battery went to the Fifty-first New York's colorbearer, as the Twenty-first's color sergeant had fallen into a deep water pit and could not extricate himself in time.[232]

About the time the Twenty-first stormed over the battery's walls, the Ninth New York was rushing over the battery from the other side, but it had not been any easier. When Flockton's bugle blew, the Ninth New York was two sections. Those men following Major Kimball were passing on to the road, crossing over the field near Porter's gunners, when the Tenth Connecticut rose up and fired a volley. The startled Zouaves, seeing the Connecticut regiment's gray overcoats, opened a scattered, scared volley; fortunately, the rifles were "fired in every direction but the right one." The Zouave officers cleared up the momentary hesitation by ordering their men on. The Tenth Connecticut, for its part, cheered on the charging Zouaves and prepared to join them.[233]

In the swamp, with the other half of the regiment, Colonel Hawkins attempted to catch up with his charging men by making his best speed through the swamp to the roadway. Breaking out of the woods and splashing through the swamp, Hawkins's column was cheered on by an excited de Monteil. Standing on a felled tree, de Monteil cried out, "Zouaves always charge them! Charge them *mes enfants!*" One moment he was encouraging the Zouaves, and the next moment he was gone. A

Confederate sniper hit de Monteil in the forehead, killing him instantly. No one would ever question his bravery again.[234]

Hawkins's and Kimball's columns collided on the roadway, which was more of a causeway surrounded by the flooded swamp at this point. The collision again confused the Zouaves, and the men hugged the roadbed in a moment of indecision. Then, in a stentorian voice heard across the field, Edgar Kimball shouted, "What's the matter here? Charge, follow me!"

With a shout, the reunited Zouaves lurched forward into the charge, and again, their peculiar cheer started up again. Pushing up the causeway with his colors, near the end of the column, Pattison saw Maggi's column off to his left. "The fifty first New York Regt. was on the left of the battery and when they see our boys coming up in front they got up off their faces where they lay in the mud. Their Colonel tried to get them to charge in but they fell on their faces," Pattison recounted.

Coming near the battery, the Ninth—led by two officers carrying rifles, Captain Edward Jardine and Lieutenant Alma P. Webster—the Zouaves fired into the fort through the center embrasure and then veered to the right where the moat was drier. The New Yorkers circled the flank and came over near Captain Schemerhorn's abandoned eighteen-pounder Mexican War trophy. The two columns met in the middle with much hand shaking and cheering but without Major Kimball.

One of the Ninth New York captains, Captain Edward Jardine of Company G, leading the way. *From the Dennis Schurr collection.*

128

"Now, in charging at the head of the regiment, Kimball of course did not see anything in the heavens above, or on the earth beneath, but the breastworks between," wrote Charles Johnson. In doing so, as the regiment left the causeway, Kimball never saw the rather deep water hole circling around the battery. Falling in, Kimball, whom Johnson described as "being rather short and stout," went in headfirst. Bobbing up and down like a cork, Kimball lost his sword and nearly drowned. All around the hole, Zouaves passed by and even jumped over the pool, paying no attention to the floundering officer. Kimball remembered one officer keenly as he floundered and confronted him later, demanding an explanation as to why he had not stopped and aided him. The officer, Lieutenant James Fleming, a tall man who cleared the hole in one bound, defended himself by saying, "Lord, Major, I would not have helped my own father up then." Kimball did finally get out and replaced his missing sword by taking a cutlass from one of Porter's sailors. A few days later, Kimball's sword was fished out of the hole and returned to him.[235]

The Union troops found the battery empty except for equipment, a wounded body servant and several dead bodies. One cannoneer was so lifelike manning Captain Schermerhorn's twenty-four-pound piece that one of the first Zouaves over the embrasure clubbed the corpse. Lieutenant William Selden was found next to his six-pounder with a bullet hole through his head. In the serene-looking engineer's hand was a taught lanyard ready to fire his last canister charge into the oncoming Federal column. The rest of the Confederates had evacuated the area.[236]

The Confederates in the battery were beset by a multitude of problems when the final charge began. Canister rounds and shells had been expended for the larger guns, so their guns stood mute on the firing line. One of the volunteers from Wise's skirmishers the night before commandeered an ox cart to bring more ammunition back, but he had not made it more than a mile up the island before the defenders streamed passed him. The gun crews and infantry defenders had held off the Union attacks for four hours. All the artillery horses and mules had been killed. Crouching behind his men, Second Lieutenant N.G. Munro was killed while trying to encourage them. Both flanks had been turned before receiving bullets from several different angles. Captain Whitson's company had been driven back from their flanking mission on Reno's column. Wise and his men were driven back by the Twenty-third Massachusetts, which had advanced past the supporting trenches, firing into the flank of the supporting companies. Wise himself had been hit three times while fighting in the woods. A bullet had struck his right arm near the elbow. Dropping his sword, he was hit in quick succession in the right lung and leg. Wise collapsed on the swampy ground, and his men dragged him to Doctor Gordon. Gordon immediately ordered the men to place Wise on the red blanket he had wrapped around him and carry him to waiting boats at Shallowbag Bay. Gordon went with the group, and as they passed around a pond, a stray bullet hit the wounded captain in the left leg. Bleeding from four wounds, Wise was suffering. As Gordon and the group exited the field heading northward, they saw the demoralizing sight of the Confederate troops breaking and running for the rear. The battle was over. The race off the island had begun.[237]

# "Don't Fire Anymore, the Island Is Surrendered!"

A fter four hours of stalwart fighting, the battle ended in a total rout. Whitson's Company arrived at the reserve post just as the rest of the defenders streamed up from the battery. The Thirty-first North Carolina, temporarily under Lieutenant Colonel Daniel G. Fowle, stood shakily. The overshooting artillery and stray rounds had caused some casualties, and many of the men knew that their weapons were inadequate to stop the onrushing Union tide. Colonel Shaw, hurrying over from Fort Bartow, tried to steady his men, but the onrushing fugitives slammed into the reserves. As the reserves stabilized, a Union volley tore into the massed ranks. A bullet smashed into Whitson's leg, and without its commander, his company melted into the muddle; all order was lost. Fowle's men joined the rout and headed northward. Shaw and his officers were facing disaster.

Two miles from the battlefield, Major Henry Fry's reinforcements were jogging down the road when the mass fugitive mob slammed into his column. In spite of their efforts, Fry and his officers could not stem the rout. His 150 men were carried along with the routed Confederates. Like a downhill snowball, the fugitive column just got larger, sweeping all in front of it.[238]

Back at the battery, the victorious Union forces cheered themselves hoarse and fought for battlefield trophies. Confederate flags became the center of arguments and fistfights until the officers sorted the entwined humanity apart. Other soldiers started to brag about their part in the battle. The Fifty-first New York finally reunited after spending the long morning in the swamp. The Twenty-third and Twenty-seventh Massachusetts Regiments finally extricated themselves from the morass and rallied on the battery. The other regiments pulled themselves together, while the Twenty-fifth Massachusetts rearmed itself from the ammunition stores brought forward by Stevenson's Twenty-fourth Massachusetts troops.

Amid all this cheering, General Burnside arrived and conferred with his generals. The battle was only half won. They had to get the troops moving before the Confederates rallied and reestablished their defenses or, worse, escaped off the island entirely. Reno was quick to get things going forward and started his Twenty-first Massachusetts Regiment down the road. Following them was the Fifty-first New York and the Ninth New York; behind them, the rest of the brigade followed. Reno drove his men hard and, with a local black guide, soon came to a crossroad that led to Shallowbag Bay. Detaching his New York regiments in this direction to cut off any escapees, Reno continued with the rest of his troops up the island.[239]

Back at the battery, the rest of the generals were not so energetic. Parke rallied and forwarded regiments after Reno until the roads were too clogged.

Attempting to retreat with the wounded Captain Wise, a Confederate boat is overtaken by Union volleys. *From* New York Illustrated Newspaper, *March 15, 1862.*

Foster, like Reno, grabbed as many regiments as he could and started after him, but most of his men were exhausted from the day's fight. The fresh Twenty-fourth Massachusetts took the lead and soon outstripped the rest of the brigade. Along the march, Union soldiers marveled at the amount of equipment that had been strewn by the retreating Confederates as they divested themselves of anything that might slow them down. Knapsacks, canteens, clothing and guns littered the roadside. It was evident that the Confederates were in a panic.[240]

Struggling with the seriously wounded Captain Wise, Dr. Gordon made for Shallowbag Bay. Gordon hoped to find a rowboat and evacuate Wise's son to Nags Head and safety, but the odds were against them. Making it to the shoreline, Gordon and his men located a boat and pushed off into the small bay. They had not rowed one hundred yards when a company of the Ninth New York trotted up the beach. Called upon to return and surrender, Gordon and his men just rowed the harder. It was an unfortunate decision. A crashing volley from the Zouaves tore into the small boat, hitting Wise for the fifth time. Gordon ordered the rowers to stop; Wise was in desperate need of medical attention, and continuing as they were was likely to get the other men killed or wounded. Gordon surrendered and, with a white handkerchief floating, rowed back, where they were placed under guard and marched to the nearby Confederate hospital, a house owned by Samuel Jarvis.

The scene at the Jarvis farm was horrific. The unpainted house was filled to capacity. The lower floors were being utilized as surgical rooms, while upstairs, men waited to be tended. Severed limbs were piled outside the door. A white sheet hung limply out of the second-floor window. Frank Vizetelly, artist-reporter for the *Illustrated London News*, came on the scene soon after the rest of the Ninth New York arrived at the farm. Vizetelly interviewed Jarvis, who was now in one of the slave cabins behind his house. Jarvis, who Hawkins had been informed was a secessionist, watched in bewilderment as his stock succumbed to the Zouaves' hunger and his wife's flat irons were used to cook them. Queried if he owned slaves, Jarvis disconnectedly replied, "Well, I *did*, but three of 'em went to Hatteras last week, two more have run away, I don't know where, and there's one in the kitchen I'll give away if anybody wants him!" A more broken man Vizetelly had not met. Looking at the scene, Jarvis told one of the Zouaves that there could not be a person living "more tired at the sight of blood."[241]

As the two New York regiments were scooping up Confederates along the Shallowbag Bay, Reno chased after the main body up the main road toward the Rebel camps. One of the Twenty-first Massachusetts's skirmishing companies, Company E, under Captain Bradford, was in the lead. Behind the Massachusetts men came the Ninth New Jersey and Fifty-first Pennsylvania. About five miles from the battlefield, Reno's column passed a little whitewashed Baptist church. Some two hundred yards ahead of them, the road turned left. Stopping at the church to set up his headquarters, Reno cheered the men on.

Just on the other side of that turn marched Lieutenant Colonel J. Wharton Green's Second North Carolina Battalion. Having hurried the men on, Green, panting for the fight, had only passed the Thirty-first North Carolina's camp when the routed defenders surged through their ranks. Officers among the fugitive mass told Green it was a foregone conclusion: the Union forces would take the island, and he was needlessly wasting his men. Riding among the throng, Green saw Colonel Shaw and asked where to deploy his men. "I hardly know," said the shell-shocked colonel, "the day is lost." Green and his officers decided to press on. If the Second North Carolina engaged the Union forces, maybe a defensive line could be cobbled together and salvage the day. It was a long shot, but Green was willing to try.

Passing around the turn in the road, Green's five hundred men met Reno's column. The lead companies, startled by each other's appearance, opened up in ragged volleys. The Second North Carolina's company fired first but aimed poorly, its rounds spatting the ground in front of Captain Bradford's riflemen. The returning volley was not so benign. Five were killed and three wounded. With the blast, Green's lead company broke and, in the crowded road conditions, dragged the rest of Green's eight companies with them. Frustrated, Green rode back to the main Confederate camp to rally his men, but for all intents and purposes, the Battle of Roanoke Island was finished.[242]

Exhausted by their run up the island, Reno halted his brigade and rested the men. The Twenty-first Massachusetts fell back to the white church, while the Fifty-first Pennsylvania rested along the roadside. The Ninth New Jersey, having broken toward the water's edge to scoop up more prisoners, found itself atop a dune overlooking the Roanoke Sound. There, one of Reno's aides found the blown New Jerseymen reclining. Exhausted and strung out across the northern portion of the island, Reno stepped aside and let Foster's troops take the advance. Foster's men pushed forward with alacrity to finish the fight before nightfall.[243]

At 2:00 p.m., five companies of the Twenty-fourth Massachusetts, commanded by Foster himself, pushed nearly a mile past Reno's outpost when they were greeted by a horseman carrying a white flag. Two other companies had been detached to the northeastern end of the island to search for escapees. Lieutenant Colonel Daniel Fowle was sent to ask for terms. Foster was adamant: "None but those of unconditional surrender." Rebuffed by the curt reply, Fowle asked how long Shaw would have to consider such indifferent terms. "Only as long as it takes you to bring that message to Colonel Shaw and return," Foster stated flatly. Foster sent Major R.H. Stevenson of the Twenty-fourth Massachusetts as the Union representative. Both men rode the mile and a half to Shaw's camp, where Stevenson found the Confederate commander sitting by a fire warming his legs. After reading the message, Shaw stared at the fire and murmured, "I must surrender." Wondering if Stevenson would relay Shaw's acceptance and his sword, Major Stevenson flatly stated, "No sir; General Foster will be here in a very short time to receive it in person." Dejected, Shaw quickly signed his acceptance to the note and sent Fowle and Stevenson back. As Stevenson left, Shaw called his orderlies to pass the news that the island was surrendered.[244]

As Stevenson and Fowle passed along the road toward Foster and his troops, they passed Green's rallied regiment, forming ranks and preparing for another battle with the Union advance. Not privy to Shaw's plans, Green was embarrassed as Fowle rode by crying out, "Don't fire any more, the island is surrendered!" Feeling betrayed by Shaw's perceived cowardice, Green marched his men back into the main Confederate camp behind Fort Huger and began to destroy their rifles.[245]

Green's troops forming in his front and Stevenson's delayed return worried Foster. Were the Confederates buying time to make a stand, attack or evacuate the island? Looking over the depleted Twenty-fourth Massachusetts, Foster called out to Colonel Stevenson, "He is gone too long; move your column forward!" The Massachusetts troops began to march toward the Confederate camp with the Twenty-third and the Twenty-seventh Massachusetts Regiments in close support. Foster's attack, however, was forestalled by Fowle's white flag, and with that, the Union troops formally accepted Shaw's surrender.[246]

The news of the surrender took time to travel, but fortunately, none of the Confederate forces were in the mood to continue the fight. In the Thirty-first North Carolina's camp, Reno's refreshed brigade took charge of the troops there as Foster marched on Shaw's camp. The Thirty-first, in its demoralized state, offered no resistance, and Colonel Jordan quietly surrendered his men.[247]

Along the western shore, the Virginians still sported some fight, but a simple action by some newspaper correspondents convinced them

The last action at the Battle of Roanoke Island was the destruction of the CSS *Curlew* by its crew on the night of the eighth. *From* Frank Leslie's Illustrated Newspaper, *March 22, 1862.*

differently. Lieutenant Colonel Anderson rallied the two Virginian regiments there and was planning to attack Foster's troops as they advanced on Shaw's camp but was surprised when the flagpole of nearby Fort Blanchard suddenly sported a Union flag. Reporter Henry Bentley of the *Philadelphia Inquirer* and artist Frank Schell of *Frank Leslie's Illustrated Newspaper* had followed the Union advance from the three-gun battery, but with the logjam of troops to the north end, the two reporters decided to cross over to the island's western coast and witness the action there. Finding a road that left the main road, they soon approached the area near Fort Blanchard. Still under the occasional naval shell, Blanchard was otherwise quiet. On further investigation, the two reporters found the fort deserted. They then put a small U.S. flag that one of them carried up the fort flagpole; seeing this, the U.S. Navy ships celebrated by blowing their steam whistles. The surprised Confederates, believing they were already surrounded, decided to give up the fight and surrendered with the North Carolinians.[248]

Fort Bartow, which had withstood a day and a half of naval bombardment, was empty as well. Union forces crept over the fort's wall just before nightfall. The crews had attempted to disable the guns, but it proved ineffective. The last island fort, the two-gun battery, fell to Company I of the Ninth New York. As the Zouaves rushed the fort, they found one Confederate, sitting by a fire and smoking a pipe, who had been left behind when there was no room in the departing boat. Later that night, the area was rocked by a large explosion as Fort Forrest and the *Curlew* were blown up by the Confederates, who melted into the mainland swamps. The Battle of Roanoke Island was over.[249]

# 14

# "At Last the Tide of Fortune Has Changed"

The haul was impressive and more than just war material. Nearly 2,500 men were captured; forty-two heavy cannons, three thousand small arms and various camp equipment, as well as two large permanent camps with hospitals, had fallen to the Union forces. The island was a ready-made base for Union operations—all for very minimal casualties; the Union had suffered 37 killed, 214 wounded and 13 missing. Two days later, Rowan's ships tracked down Lynch's Mosquito Fleet at Elizabeth City and, in a short battle, destroyed the last vestiges of Confederate naval power in North Carolina.[250] Several of the cities along the Albemarle Sound surrendered without a shot being fired. As planned, the victory laid bare North Carolina's interior to Burnside's troops.

All portions of Burnside's plan paid dividends. A new working relationship with the navy prompted continued close partnerships. Burnside's Expedition became the blueprint for continuing naval ventures, such as actions on the Mississippi River and later attacks on Fort Fisher near Wilmington, North Carolina.[251] The idea was so well accepted that it became army/navy doctrine, realized to a larger scale in World War II with the Pacific Campaign and Normandy Landings.

The fifteen correspondents whom Burnside imbedded with his troops also proved their worth. The correspondents, including two for English newspapers, wrote of the overwhelming Union victory. Their articles and opinions rallied an incredulous Northern population, while it tamped down war talk in Europe and buoyed flagging Union war morale, which, like the

Surrendered Confederates presented a wide assortment of armaments and uniforms, as portrayed in this image. *From* New York Illustrated Newspaper, *March 15, 1862.*

spring, was reawakening. The Battle of Roanoke had been the first major victory in the war's eastern theater. With the Battle of Roanoke Island and Ulysses S. Grant's victories in Tennessee at the same time, the Union populace began to believe again. Recruitment for old regiments, which had slackened, was back up to acceptable levels, while new regiments began to be organized in large numbers. The coordination between the navy and army showed the efficiency of the Northern military, dispelling the inferiority of the summer before. The lack of supplies for and the condition of the Confederate garrison also showed the initial progress of the naval blockade. An ebullient North had shed the inadequacy of 1861 and girded on the armor for the long war ahead in full realization that victory was achievable.

*London Illustrated Newspaper* artist and writer Frank Vizetelly expounded on the success of Roanoke Island. "At last the tide of fortune has turned in favour of the North," Vizetelly wrote on February 28 to his readers. "The victories in North Carolina, Kentucky and Tennessee, have dealt a staggering blow at secession; while the Federal troops, hitherto depressed by their earlier discomforts, are now elated and confident." It was a signal victory that changed the very soul of the Union and its army. In

Great Britain, the pro-Southern forces, who had been railing to break the blockade and arbitrate the conflict during the Trent Affair, found public opinion had shifted once again. Britons were no longer interested in becoming involved in an American war with a North that was now fully ready for battle. Diplomatically, the American war was dividing Europe as well. While France was pro-Southern, Russia, Prussia and some other nations were publicly supportive of the North. Great Britain, which could little afford to be involved in a continental war, decided to remain neutral, and the new ambassadors from the Confederacy were soon denied access to the Court of St. James.[252]

France, led by Ambassador Mercier, continued to rail for intervention, but without Great Britain's aid, France did not feel comfortable engaging the North alone. Without the British fleet, France could only diplomatically press for arbitration. Lincoln's administration largely ignored the demands, and by the summer of 1862, France decided to become embroiled in Mexican politics directly. The ensuing Mexican Adventure would end in ruin for the French, but in 1862, they simply abandoned any direct involvement in the U.S. Civil War.[253]

The Confederate press could not conceal the extent of the disaster. Nearly 2,500 soldiers had been captured, many without firing a shot, forty-two cannons lost and a fleet destroyed. It didn't seem possible. Wise was blamed initially for the failure, so an investigation was called, and Wise, who had kept all his orders, went on the attack. Wise would prove conclusively that Huger and War Secretary Judah Benjamin had wantonly left the post poorly defended. With the populace siding with the grieving father, Wise would be exonerated of any blame, forcing Benjamin to resign and Huger to be shelved instead. But the real damage was done. As Wise, Hill and others had predicted, the fall of Roanoke Island threatened Confederate resources.[254]

Burnside's campaign would be successful for the spring. His men would capture New Bern in March and then Fort Macon and Beaufort in April. Despite all of Huger's actions, Norfolk fell to Union forces in May. By June, Burnside would be preparing for an overland march on Wilmington when the war to the north took a change. McClellan's attack, which started the month after Roanoke Island, had gotten to with eight miles of Richmond when the Confederate army came out of its trenches and, in a serious of vicious attacks, drove his army to the James River's shore. Believing he was outnumbered, McClellan ordered Burnside to take all his available troops and join him. Burnside soon left North Carolina with nearly ten thousand men, leaving Foster behind to garrison the victories of the spring. The unfinished campaign was deemed a partial success.[255]

One result that neither side foresaw involved the African American slaves. Burnside had been told not to talk about the slaves, but with so many New England regiments in his army, he wasn't going to return them either. Upon landing on Roanoke Island, Burnside confiscated the Confederate army's two hundred laborers, treating them legally as Confederacy military equipment. He then freed the slaves, giving them three choices: be resettled in the North, work on the island for wages or return to slavery. Most of the men returned willingly to slavery, if only to rescue family members, returning to the island and freedom by the end of February. Their actions encouraged others to seek freedom as well, and with the belief that Union forces ensured emancipation, thousands of slaves made the trek to Union lines. Soon contrabands, literally meaning war material, were placed in camps behind Union lines. The freed slaves provided a steady workforce, constructing Union fortifications and wharves and loading and unloading supplies at miltiary depots. After the Emancipation Proclamation's passage, many of this workforce became Union soldiers, thousands in North Carolina fielding in the army and navy. They also provided information and acted as guides and spies against their former masters. With their departure, the Confederacy's ability to produce many foodstuffs suffered, further hampering the Confederacy's ability to carry on the war.[256]

But the largest success was lifting Lincoln's depression. As the Union leader, it was important for him to believe in himself because the Union populace would take its cues from his outward appearance. Two days before the battle, a cheerful President Lincoln greeted his old friend Joshua Speed. Judge Speed was surprised at Lincoln's emotional change. Lincoln explained that with the forthcoming campaign, including Burnside's Expedition, "he was now in great hopes that the rebellion would pretty much be ended." Before Roanoke Island, the Union was in danger of collapse. The populace, and even its leadership, was demoralized; the army seemed emasculated; and European powers were poised to intervene in the South's favor. Now, the nation and the army were emboldened, European powers were cowed and the war seemed winnable. Lincoln, who a month before had worried that he would be the last president of the United States, now felt that the light at the end of the tunnel was visible. There would be difficult times ahead, but as Lincoln wrote, it was for the North to "nobly save or meanly lose, the last best hope on earth."[257]

# Appendix

## Union Army

### *Coast Division (Brigadier General Ambrose E. Burnside)*

First Brigade (Brigadier General John G. Foster)
Tenth Connecticut, Colonel Charles L. Russell
Twenty-third Massachusetts, Colonel John Kurtz
Twenty-fourth Massachusetts (seven companies), Colonel Thomas G. Stevenson
Twenty-fifth Massachusetts, Colonel Edwin Upton
Twenty-seventh Massachusetts, Colonel Horace C. Lee

Second Brigade (Brigadier General Jesse L. Reno)
Twenty-first Massachusetts, Lieutenant Colonel Alberto R. Maggi
Ninth New Jersey, Lieutenant Colonel Charles A. Heckman
Fifty-first New York, Colonel Edward Ferrero
Fifty-first Pennsylvania, Colonel John F. Hartranft

Third Brigade (Brigadier General John G. Parke)
Eighth Connecticut, Colonel Edward Harland
Eleventh Connecticut (not in Battle of Roanoke Island)

Ninth New York, Colonel Rush C. Hawkins
Fourth Rhode Island, Colonel Isaac P. Rodman
Fifth Rhode Island, Major John Wright

Unassigned Units
First New York Marine Artillery (detachment), Colonel William A. Howard
Ninety-ninth New York (Union Coast Guard), Lieutenant Charles W. Tillotson

## Division of Armed Vessels

Captain Samuel F. Hazard
Army gunboats:
*Picket*, Captain Thomas P. Ives
*Vidette*, Captain John L. Foster
*Hussar*, Captain Frederick Crocker
*Lancer*, Captain M.B. Morley
*Ranger*, Captain Samuel Emmerson
*Chasseur*, Captain John West
*Pioneer*, Captain Charles E. Baker
*Sentinel*

# UNION NAVY

Flag Officer: L.M. Goldsborough
Chief of the Staff: Commander A.L. Case
Staff Medical Officer: Assistant Surgeon S.C. Jones
Signal Officer: H.G.B. Fisher
Secretary to Flag Officer: Henry Van Brunt
Clerk to Flag Officer: E.C. Meeker
Second Clerk to Flag Officer: S.C. Rowan

# Vessels of the Squadron

Flagship, steam gunboat *Philadelphia*
    Acting Master: S. Reynolds
    Lieutenant: E.L. Haines, of Philadelphia
    Chief Engineer: Charles A. Norris, of Washington
    Assistants: Charles R. Joyce and A.J. Hopkins, of Washington
    Acting Purser: T. Thornton
steam gunboat *Stars and Stripes*, Lieutenant Commanding R. Worden
steam gunboat *Valley City*, Lieutenant Commanding J.C. Chaplin
steam gunboat *Underwriter*, Lieutenant Commanding W.V. Jeffers
steam gunboat *Hetzel*, Lieutenant Commanding H. K. Davenport
steam gunboat *Delaware*, Lieutenant Commanding S.P. Quackenbush
steam gunboat *Shawsheen*, Acting Master T.G. Woodward
steam gunboat *Lockwood*, Acting Master G.L. Graves
steam gunboat *Ceres*, Acting Master J. McDiarmid
steam gunboat *Morse*, Acting Master Peter Hayes
steam gunboat *Whitehead*, Acting Master Charles A. French
steam gunboat *Virginia*
steam gunboat *Louisiana*, Lieutenant Commanding A. Murray
steam gunboat *Henry Brincker*, Acting Master Commanding John E. Geddings
steam gunboat *General Putnam*, Lieutenant Commanding McCook
steam gunboat *Hunchback*, Acting Lieutenant Commanding E.R. Calhoun
steam gunboat *Southfield*, Volunteer Lieutenant Commanding C.F.W. Beam
steam gunboat *Young America*
steam gunboat *Commodore Barney*, Acting Lieut Commanding R.D. Renshaw
steam gunboat *Commodore Perry*, Acting Lieutenant Commanding Charles
    W. Fluster
sailing gunboat *J.N. Seymour*
sailing gunboat *Granite*, Acting Master Commanding Ephraim Boomer
sailing gunboat *Jenny Lind*

From *Rebellion Record*, vol. 4, 1862, 89.

# CONFEDERATE ARMY

Brigadier General Henry A. Wise (not present in battle; ill)
  Colonel Henry M. Shaw, second in command
  Eighth North Carolina, Colonel Henry M. Shaw
  Seventeenth North Carolina (three companies), Major Gabriel H. Hill
  Thirty-first North Carolina, Colonel John V. Jordan

## *Wise Legion*

Second North Carolina Battalion, Lieutenant Colonel Wharton J. Green
Forty-sixth Virginia, Lieutenant Major Henry W. Fry
Fifty-ninth Virginia, Colonel Frank P. Anderson

# CONFEDERATE NAVY

## *Mosquito Fleet (Flag Officer William F. Lynch)*

Flagship, *Sea Bird*, Lieutenant Commander Patrick McCarrick
*Curlew* (sunk), Captain Thomas T. Hunter
*Ellis*, Lieutenant James W. Cooke
*Beaufort*, Lieutenant Commander William Harwar Pat
*Raleigh*, Lieutenant Commander Joseph W. Alexander
*Fanny*, Midshipman James Langhorne Tayloe
*Forrest*, Lieutenant Commander James L. Hoole
*Appomattox* (not at Battle of Roanoke Island), Lieutenant Charles C. Simms
schooner *Black Warrior*, Lieutenant Frank M. Harris

From *Battles and Leaders*, vol. 1, 670.

# Notes

## CHAPTER 1

1. While numerous books mention Lincoln's melancholy throughout the war, Michael Burlingame's *The Inner World of Abraham Lincoln*, 104–6, covers the ups and downs that the war displayed in Lincoln's emotions better than most.
2. Davis, *Battle at Bull Run*.
3. Foote, *Civil War*, 92–95.
4. Ibid., 104–9.
5. Burlingame, *Abraham Lincoln: A Life*, vol. 2, 199–200; Linn, *Horace Greeley*, 191.
6. Linn, *Horace Greeley*, 190–91.
7. Ibid., 193–95.
8. Goodwin, *Team of Rivals*, 354–55.
9. George Hollis Papers, "Battle of Roanoke Island."
10. Siegel, "British Foreign Policy."
11. Foote, *Civil War*, 156–57.
12. Bancroft, *Life of William*, vol. 2, 137.
13. Siegel, "British Foreign Policy."
14. Burlingame, *Abraham Lincoln: A Life*, vol. 2, 220.

## CHAPTER 2

15. Sauers, *Succession*, 117–19.
16. Cullen, "Very Beau Ideal," 4.
17. Poore, *Life and Public*, 27–30.
18. Ibid., 29–89.
19. Sauers, *Succession*, 22–23.
20. Graham, *Ninth Regiment*, 78–81.
21. Sauers, *Succession*, 22, 41.
22. Croffut and Morris, *Military History*, 122–25. For African Americans in the Eighth Connecticut, see *Pine & Palm*, November 11, 1861, "Self Defenders of Connecticut."
23. Alduino and Coles, *Sons of Garibaldi*, 85–89.
24. Denny, *Wearing the Blue*, 10–12.
25. Croffut and Morris, *Military History*, 125–28.
26. Derby, *Bearing Arms*, 7, 16, 19–24, 34–35.
27. Valentine, *Story of Company*, 20–22.
28. Sauers, ed., *Civil War Journal*, 13–37. Hartranft and his Pennsylvanians of the Fifty-first were not the only regiment or battery that left at the end of their enlistment.
29. Troiani, Coates and McAfee. *Don Troiani's Regiments*, 82–83.
30. Wheeler and Pitt, "Fifty-third New York," 415–16.
31. Walcott, *History*, 1, 10–15.
32. Ibid., 10, 16–18.
33. Roe, *Twenty-fourth*, 9–35.
34. Croffut and Morris, *Military History*, 128; Burlingame, *History of the Fifth*, 1–7.
35. Chase, *Battery F*, 1–14.
36. Sauers, *Succession*, 50–51.
37. Ibid., 64–66.
38. Ibid., 66.
39. Ibid.
40. Allen, *Forty-six Months*, 13–42.
41. Drake, *History*, 7–22.
42. Sauers, *Succession*, 109–11.

# Chapter 3

43. *Philadelphia Inquirer*, "The Burnside Expedition," December 10, 1861.

44. George Hollis Papers, "Battle of Roanoke Island."

45. Emmerton, *Record*, 28–29.

46. Denny, *Wearing the Blue*, 45; Croffut and Morris, *Military History*, 162–63.

47. Derby, *Bearing Arms*, 41–42, 45–46.

48. Walcott, *History*, 19–21.

49. Sauers, *Succession*, 108–9, 113; Andrews, *North Reports*, 219; Jackman, *History of the Sixth*, 1–20.

50. Sauers, *Succession*, 113, 117.

51. Ibid., 108–9.

52. *Philadelphia Inquirer*, February 11, 1861; July 1, 1861; March 4, 1862; Sauers, *Succession*, 47.

53. Sauers, *Succession*, 4, 117.

54. Ibid., 117.

55. Day, *My Diary*, 18; Jackman, *History of the Sixth*, 21.

56. Jackman, *History of the Sixth*, 21–22.

57. Wheeler and Pitt, "Fifty-third New York," 416–17; Sauers, *Succession*, 56.

58. Sauers, *Succession*, 29–30; U.S. Naval War Records Office, *Official Records*, vol. 6, 581–82 (hereafter referred to as ORN).

59. George Hollis Papers, "Battle of Roanoke Island."

60. Moore, ed., *Rebellion Record*, 80–81.

# Chapter 4

61. Trotter, *Ironclads*, 1–3; Powell, *North Carolina*, 1–4. The Outer Banks are 175 miles long; the remaining coast is the same distance.

62. U.S. Bureau of Census, *Population Schedules*, vol. 2; Bassett, *Slavery*, 66–71.

63. Trotter, *Ironclads*, 1–3; Barrett, *Civil War*, 68–69.

64. Harper, *History of Chesapeake*, 126–27.

65. Powell, *North Carolina*, 345–48.

66. Barrett, *Civil War*, 17–21.

67. Ibid., 61.

68. Trotter, *Ironclads*, 33–40.

69. Barrett, *Civil War*, 51–55.

70. Daley, "Burnside's Amphibious Division," 30–31.

71. Barrett, *Civil War*, 67.

72. Stillwell, "General Hawkins," 70, 86–88.

73. Graham, *Ninth Regiment*, 8–10, 12.

74. Whitney, *Hawkins Zouaves*, 66.

75. Sauers, *Succession*, 26–36.

76. Ibid., 35–37.

77. Johnson and Buell, *Battles*, vol. 2, 121.

78. Sauers, *Succession*, 115–17.

79. Wise, *Life of Henry*, 16–121.

80. Wise, *End of an Era*, 165–74.

81. Trotter, *Ironclads*, 64; Sauers, *Succession*, 98, 152.

82. William W. Turner, "First Twelve Months of the Third Georgia Regiment," (Putnam County, GA) *Countryman*, 1864.

83. Wise, *End of an Era*, 175, 181; Click, *Time Full of Trial*, 24.

84. Turner, "First Twelve Months"; War Department. U.S. War Department, *War of the Rebellion*, vol. 4, 655 (hereafter referred to as OR). The fort was named for Colonel Francis P. Bartow of the Sixth Georgia.

85. Turner, "First Twelve Months." First called Sturgis' Battery by the Third Georgia, the three-gun battery was named Fort Defiance and Fort/Battery Russell. To avoid confusion, it will be called the three-gun battery.

86. Barrett, *Civil War*, 74; Sauers, *Succession*, 90.

87. Bridges, *Lee's Maverick General*, 22–23, 30–31.

88. U.S. War Department, *War of the Rebellion*, vol. 4, ser. 1, 682.

89. Sauers, *Succession*, 94–95.

90. Hill, *North Carolina*, vol. 1, 186; *New York Herald*, "Sketches of the Rebel Officers," February 16, 1862; Parker, *Recollections of a Naval Officer*, 222–26.

91. Trotter, *Ironclads*, 62, 64; Sauers, *Succession*, 96.

92. Trotter, *Ironclads*, 63–64.

93. OR, vol. 9, 113, 129.

94. Ibid., 126–27.

95. Ibid., 133; Green, *Recollections*, 154.

96. Trotter, *Ironclads*, 66; Sauers, *Succession*, 153.

97. OR, vol. 9, 133.

98. Wise, *End of an Era*, 173; OR, vol. 9, 145–47; Sauers, *Succession*, 161.

99. Sauers, *Succession*, 151.

100. OR, vol. 9, 150–51.

101. Wise, *Life of Henry*, 309.

# CHAPTER 5

102. Moore, ed., *Rebellion Record*, 81.
103. Burlingame, *History of the Fifth*, 11–12.
104. Walcott, *History*, 21–22.
105. Day, *My Diary*, 21.
106. George Hollis Papers, "Battle of Roanoke Island."
107. Sauers, *Succession*, 122–23; *(Washington, D.C.) National Tribune*, March 21, 1889.
108. Moore, ed., *Rebellion Record*, 82.
109. Ibid., 82–84.
110. Sauers, *Succession*, 125–26; Moore, ed., *Rebellion Record*, 85, 88; Denny, *Wearing the Blue*, 59; ORN, vol. 6, 582.
111. Putnam, *Story*, 50–51; Emmerton, *Record*, 36; Denny, *Wearing the Blue*, 59; Day, *My Diary*, 22.
112. Barrett, *Civil War*, 70.
113. Drake, *History*, 26–27; Moore, ed., *Rebellion Record*, 85.
114. Moore, ed., *Rebellion Record*, 85.
115. Ibid., 85.
116. Sauers, *Succession*, 131.
117. Drake, *History*, 35–38; Moore, ed., *Rebellion Record*, 87.
118. Daley, "Burnside's Amphibious Division," 30–31; Moore, ed., *Rebellion Record*, 88.
119. Sauers, *Succession*, 129.
120. Walcott, *History*, 24–26.
121. Sauers, *Succession*, 135–36.
122. Ibid., 132–34.
123. Ibid., 137–38.
124. Barrett, *Civil War*, 73.

# CHAPTER 6

125. Draper, *Recollections*, 48–49.
126. Wheeler and Pitt, "Fifty-third New York," 420–25.
127. Johnson, *Long Roll*, 88; Graham, *Ninth Regiment*, 32–118. Based on photographs of Ninth New York members located in the Peekskill Museum in Peekskill, New York, the Ninth received two different Zouave

uniforms. The ones described by members in their postwar writings was the later set that they wore during the Antietam Campaign.

128. Allen, *Harriet Tubman*, 96; Click, *Time Full of Trial*, 24; Johnson, *Long Roll*, 70–71, 75–76. Johnson's mentions of "Ben" probably refers to Ben Tillett, who aided the Union forces.

129. Moore, ed., *Rebellion Record*, 88–89; Click, *Time Full of Trial*, 24.

130. Click, *Time Full of Trial*, 24.

131. Day, *My Diary*, 31–32.

132. Moore, ed., *Rebellion Record*, 97; ORN, vol. 6, 552.

133. Moore, ed., *Rebellion Record*, 97; Parker, *Recollections*, 227–28.

134. Parker, *Recollections*, 228.

# CHAPTER 7

135. ORN, vol. 6, 561.

136. *Richmond (VA) Daily Dispatch*, February 27, 1862.

137. ORN, vol. 6, 552.

138. *Richmond (VA) Daily Dispatch*, February 27, 1862; ORN, vol. 6, 594.

139. ORN, vol. 6, 561–62, 552–53.

140. *Richmond (VA) Daily Dispatch*, February 27, 1862.

141. Moore, ed., *Rebellion Record*, 98.

142. *Richmond (VA) Daily Dispatch*, February 27, 1862.

143. ORN, vol. 6, 557, 568–69, 575; Blanding, *Recollections*, 104.

144. ORN, vol. 6, 555–56.

145. Moore, ed., *Rebellion Record*, 101.

146. ORN, vol. 6, 558–59.

147. Ibid., 564–65.

148. Owens, "Confederate Flag," 116–18. While the article suggests the event occurred on the eighth, it is more than likely the events happened on the seventh, as Fort Bartow only saw limited action on the eighth.

149. Moore, ed., *Rebellion Record*, 100.

150. Sauers, *Succession*, 169.

151. *Richmond (VA) Daily Dispatch*, February 27, 1862.

152. *Richmond (VA) Daily Dispatch*, February 27, 1862; OR, vol. 9, 179; Green, *Recollections*, 155.

153. *Richmond (VA) Daily Dispatch*, February 19, 1862; ORN, vol. 6, 595–96; Parker, *Recollections of a Naval Officer, 1841–1865*, 229. Parker establishes the sequence of

events used here: *Forrest* was incapacitated on the first attack and *Curlew* on the second. *Forrest* was named for Confederate naval district officer French Forrest.

154. Moore, ed., *Rebellion Record*, 100.

155. OR, vol. 9, 150–51.

156. Ibid., 170–71.

157. Payne, *Place Names*, 17; U.S. Bureau of Census, *Population Schedules*, vol. 5, 121. According to most sources, the landing site was named the Hammond, Haimen or Hammon House. This was a mispronunciation of the local name Hayman, members of which family still reside on the island. The house still stands.

158. OR, vol. 9, 171.

159. Ibid., 176.

160. Burlingame, *History of the Fifth*, 22.

# CHAPTER 8

161. Moore, ed., *Rebellion Record*, 100.

162. OR, vol. 9, 76, 86; Moore, ed., *Rebellion Record*, 96; While Reno may have written the debarkation orders, the plan shows Foster's engineering talents.

163. Moore, ed., *Rebellion Record*, 96.

164. Ibid.; OR, vol. 9, 76, 86, 98.

165. ORN, vol. 9, 76, 176, 563–64; Moore, ed., *Rebellion Record*, 101; OR, vol. 9, 76, 176.

166. OR, vol. 9, 76.

167. Smith W. Higgins, "The First Flag Planted on Roanoke Island," *(Washington, D.C.) National Tribune*, May 17, 1883; W.G. Bartholomew, "A Fighting Regiment's First Battle," *(Washington, D.C.) National Tribune*, October 10, 1901; Derby, *Bearing Arms*, 59; Putnam, *Story*, 66–67; C.W. Putnam, "Burnside's Expedition," *(Washington, D.C.) National Tribune*, April 12, 1883; Day, *My Diary*, 34; Denny, *Wearing the Blue*, 70–72; U.S. Sanitary Commission, *Catalogue*, 81. The item is number 790.

168. Moore, ed., *Rebellion Record*, 111.

169. OR, vol. 9, 98–99; *Brooklyn (NY) Daily Eagle*, "The Fifty-first Regiment at Roanoke Island," February 27, 1862.

170. OR, vol. 9, 105.

171. Ibid., 74–76.

172. Parker, *Recollections of a Naval Officer, 1841–1865*, 229–31; ORN, vol. 6, 594–95, 597.

173. ORN, vol. 6, 594–95, 597.

174. OR, vol. 9, 86, 98, 105; Walcott, *History*, 41. The one casualty was Private Henry H. Howard, who was wounded in the hips.

175. Whitney, *Hawkins Zouaves*, 71; OR, vol. 9, 77.

176. OR, vol. 9, 100–101.

177. Ibid., 171, 174, 177.

178. Ibid., 179; Thomas Dolan, "Fight at Roanoke Island," *Raleigh (NC) Weekly Standard*, February 26, 1862.

179. Johnson, *Long Roll*, 91.

180. Graham, *Ninth Regiment*, 125.

181. Whitney, *Hawkins Zouaves*, 72.

182. Moore, ed., *Rebellion Record*, 111.

# CHAPTER 9

183. OR, vol. 9, 77, 86, 98, 105.

184. Ibid., 83; Croffut and Morris, *Military History*, 681.

185. Moore, ed., *Rebellion Record*, 111.

186. Abbott, "Heroic Deeds," 559–71; OR, vol. 9, 96, 101. The column passed Maggi's outposts at 7:30 a.m.

187. Putnam, *Story*, 67–71; Moore, ed., *Rebellion Record*, 111; OR, vol. 9, 96. Putnam of Company A in the Twenty-fifth Massachusetts also mentions crossing the creek three times and describes the depth as waist high.

188. Dolan, "Fight at Roanoke Island"; OR, vol. 9, 180.

189. OR, vol. 9, 101; Walcott, *History*, 32; Burlingame, *History of the Fifth*, 23.

190. Putnam, *Story*, 72–75; Parkhurst, *Proceedings*. Since the whole work deals with this part of the battle, no specific pages have been notated.

191. OR, vol. 9, 96; Day, *My Diary*, 35; Denny, *Wearing the Blue*, 73–74; Putnam, *Story*, 71–73.

192. Day, *My Diary*, 35–36; OR, vol. 9, 83. Fortunately for all involved, Dr. Rice was only bruised by the musket ball.

193. Emmerton, *Record*, 49; Bartholomew, "Fighting Regiment's."

194. OR, vol. 9, 87; Parkhurst, *Proceedings*, 36–55. Parkhurst says that his company and two others were forced to withdraw "to the left" because of the situation. By the time they retreated, the Tenth Connecticut had taken over for the Twenty-fifth Massachusetts.

195. Moore, ed., *Rebellion Record*, 112.

# CHAPTER 10

196. OR, vol. 9, 101.

197. *Randolph (MA) Transcript*, March 8, 1862; Johnson, *Long Roll*, 92–93.

198. OR, vol. 9, 101.

199. *Randolph (MA) Transcript*, March 8, 1862; OR, 101.

200. OR, vol. 9, 102–103.

201. Ibid., 104; Parker, *History of the Fifty-first*, 77.

202. OR, vol. 9, 101; Lewis, "Our Army Correspondence from a Roxbury Boy," *Roxbury (MA) City Gazette*, March 6, 1862.

203. Burlingame, *History of the Fifth*, 24; Long, *Five*, 106.

204. OR, vol. 9, 83.

205. Roe, *Twenty-fourth*, 59–60.

206. OR, vol. 9, 106.

# CHAPTER 11

207. OR, vol. 9, 180; "Sketches of the Rebel Officers." Anderson had served in the mercenary campaigns in Nicaragua under William Walker in the 1850s.

208. OR, vol. 9, 166. Wise's report contradicts Anderson and says the three companies were split on the flanks of the battery.

209. Ibid., 170–74; Sauers, *Succession*, 160. Selden's censure stems from disagreement with Wise on the obstruction/piling line's placement and its incomplete status on the eve of the battle.

210. Ibid., 174–78.

211. Ibid., 177–78. They were led up from the reserve by Major Lawson of the Fifty-ninth Virginia.

212. Ibid., 172.

213. W.E. Doyle, "Confederate Surgeon's Narrative of His Capture and the Death of Captain Wise," *(Washington, D.C.) National Tribune*, December 12, 1895.

214. OR, vol. 9, 156, 179. Wise felt that Fry delayed his departure and waited too long to land his men, ensuring their capture.

215. Green, *Recollections*, 157; OR, vol. 9, 178.

216. ORN, vol. 6, 549; Bohemian, "Battle of Roanoke Island," *Richmond (VA) Daily Dispatch*, February 27–28, 1862.

217. OR, vol. 9, 174.

218. Moore, ed., *Rebellion Record*, 115.

# CHAPTER 12

219. Moore, ed., *Rebellion Record*, 104; James H. Rogers, "Roanoke Island—What a Green Regiment Did in that Action," *(Washington, D.C.) National Tribune*, August 7, 1890; Whitney, *Hawkins Zouaves*, 74.

220. Whitney, *Hawkins Zouaves*, 74.

221. OR, vol. 9, 106; Johnson, *Long Roll*, 93; National Archives, John William Pattison Pension.

222. Johnson, *Long Roll*, 93–95; Denny, *Wearing the Blue*, 75; Sauers, *Succession*, 195. Without getting too involved in the Ninth New York at Roanoke Island controversy, there are various factors that caused the nearly forty year writing war between the regiments: 1. No newspapermen were with the flanking parties and therefore only viewed the battlefield from the southern edge of the field (i.e., behind the Ninth New York). 2. As it was the first real victory for the North, *every* regiment wanted to be the regiment that won the battle. 3. As time passed after the event, few survivors remembered fully or correctly.

223. Johnson, *Long Roll*, 94–95; *New York Herald*, "The Capture of Roanoke Island," March 2, 1862. A fellow zouave sheepishly admitted that they fired into the Ninth New Jersey but said the firing was almost immediately halted.

224. Graham, *Ninth Regiment*, 139–40.

225. OR, vol. 9, 87, 106; Johnson, *Long Roll*, 95; D.L. McKay, "Roanoke and New Berne," *(Washington, D.C.) National Tribune*, November 20, 1884; Frank Vizetelly, "The Federal Victory at Roanoke Island," *London Illustrated Newspaper*, March 22, 1862. Vizetelly suggests the officer was Lieutenant Selden.

226. Whitney, *Hawkins Zouaves*, 74.

227. Ibid., 75; Johnson, *Long Roll*, 95; National Archives, John William Pattison Pension.

228. Emmerton, *Record*, 49; Bartholomew, "Fighting Regiment's."

229. Drake, *History*, 44–45; "Fifty-first Regiment"; OR, vol. 9, 104. Here is an occasion where heliocentric problems arise. Most regiments mention that the conditions were too foggy/smoky to see effectively, yet the sky clears in Drake's account only for the Ninth New Jersey. Drake also reiterates the same printed arguments that the Ninth New York fired on the Union troops in multiple volleys but, in the same instant, quotes Captain Otis of the Tenth Connecticut, stating the Ninth New York broke up and fired scattered shots in all directions except the right one. He then suggests that Burnside ordered the Zouaves out of the department because of their poor control, when in reality, the Ninth New York was taken to Virginia with

other regiments that became the core of Burnside's Ninth Corps. In the earlier *Brooklyn (NY) Daily Eagle* article, a lieutenant from the Fifty-first New York mentions that the Ninth New Jersey fired volleys into his regiment, displaying the great confusion that reigned that day. Ferrero's remaining companies were eventually forced to lie down in the mud "to avoid the shower of bullets from our own troops as well as those from the enemy."

230. Charles Miller letter in *Randolph (MA) Transcript*; Lewis, "Our Army."

231. Walcott, *History*, 34. Stearns was also a confidant to the poet Emily Dickinson.

232. OR, vol. 9, 101; Lewis, "Our Army"; George P. Howes, "From Alert Comrades Along the Whole Line," *(Washington, D.C.) National Tribune*, December 30, 1897; "Fifty-first Regiment."

233. Emmerton, *Record*, 50; Whitney, *Hawkins Zouaves*, 74–75. Here is another dichotomy: many in the Ninth New Jersey claim they were hit by three well-aimed volleys, yet the Ninth New York fired only a scattered volley from that portion of the battlefield. The other volleys must have come from the Tenth Connecticut.

234. Graham, *Ninth Regiment*, 139–40. So vitriolic were the claims and counterclaims on who did what in this battle that many regimental historians made veiled accusations that the Ninth New York accidentally killed de Monteil. See Emmerton, *Record*, 50.

235. John H.E. Whitney, "Hawkins Zouaves," *(Washington, D.C.) National Tribune*, May 3, 1888; Graham, *Ninth Regiment*, 141; National Archives, John William Pattison Pension; Johnson, *Long Roll*, 99–100.

236. Johnson, *Long Roll*, 95; Walcott, *History*, 35.

237. Dolan, "Fight at Roanoke Island"; OR, vol. 9, 174; Emmerton, *Record*, 49; Doyle, "Confederate Surgeon's Narrative."

# Chapter 13

238. OR, vol. 9, 172–73, 175, 179.

239. Ibid., 101, 103. Reno's guide was Ben Tillett.

240. Ibid., 88, 107; Roe, *Twenty-fourth*, 61.

241. Doyle, "Confederate Surgeon's Narrative"; Vizetelly, "Federal Victory"; Johnson, *Long Roll*, 97.

242. Walcott, *History*, 49; Green, *Recollections*, 157–58. The only real open space near this skirmish was the Baptist Church, which still stands. See William B. Franklin's 1852 map.

243. OR, vol. 9, 88.

244. Barrett, *Civil War*, 83–84.

245. Green, *Recollections*, 158.

246. Barrett, *Civil War*, 84.

247. OR, vol. 9, 102.

248. Andrews, *North Reports*, 220.

249. OR, vol. 9, 107; Johnson, *Long Roll*, 96–97; Sauers, *Succession*, 199. The Fourth Rhode Island and Tenth Connecticut captured the abandoned Fort Bartow.

# Chapter 14

250. Sauers, *Succession*, 200–202; Moore, ed., *Rebellion Record*, 122–23.

251. For a greater understanding of army/naval actions, see Hinds, *Invasion*.

252. Vizetelly, "Federal Victory"; Jones, "Britain's Surrogate."

253. Bancroft, *Life of William*, vol. 2, 137, 298–99.

254. For details and the outcome of the Confederate investigation on the Fall of Roanoke Island, see Confederate States Government, *Report*.

255. Sauers, *Succession*, 441–62.

256. See Click, *Time Full of Trial*, for the story of African Americans on Roanoke Island.

257. *New York Tribune*, "Washington Correspondence," February 7, 1862; Lincoln, "Annual Message."

# Bibliography

## Primary

Allen, George H. *Forty-six Months with the Fourth R.I. Volunteers in the War of 1861 to 1865.* Providence, RI: J.A. and R.A. Reid, 1887.

Amory, Charles B. *A Brief Record of the Army Life of Charles B. Amory.* N.p.: privately published, 1902.

Avery, William B. "Marine Artillery with the Burnside Expedition and the Battle of Camden." *Personal Narratives of the Battles of the Rebellion, Being Papers Read Before the Rhode Island Soldiers and Sailors Historical Society* 2, no. 4 (1880).

Barney, Caleb H. "A Country Boy's First Three Months in the Army." *Personal Narratives of the Battles of the Rebellion, Being Papers Read Before the Rhode Island Soldiers and Sailors Historical Society* 2, no. 2 (1880).

Bates, David Homer. *Lincoln in the Telegraph Officer.* New York: Century Company, 1907.

Blanding, Stephen F. *Recollections of a Sailor Boy or the Cruise of the Gunboat Louisiana.* Providence, RI: E.A. Johnson & Company, 1886.

Burlingame, John K. *History of the Fifth Regiment Rhode Island Heavy Artillery, During Three Years and a Half Service in North Carolina.* Providence, RI: Snow & Farnham, 1892.

Burnside, Ambrose E. "The Burnside Expedition." *Personal Narratives of the Battles of the Rebellion, Being Papers Read Before the Rhode Island Soldiers and Sailors Historical Society* 2, no. 7 (1882).

Burns, William H. *My Personal Recollections of the War, 1861, 1862 and 1863*. St. Paul, MN: Railroader Print, 1923.

Chase, Philip S. *Battery F, First Rhode Island Light Artillery, in the Civil War, 1861–1865*. Providence, RI: Snow & Farnham, 1882.

Chenery, William H. "Reminiscences of the Burnside Expedition." *Personal Narratives of the Battles of the Rebellion, Being Papers Read Before the Rhode Island Soldiers and Sailors Historical Society* 7, no. 1 (1905).

Confederate States Government. *Report of the Roanoke Island Investigation Committee*. Richmond, VA: Enquirer Book and Job Press, 1862.

Day, David L. *My Diary of Rambles with the Twenty-fifth Massachusetts Volunteer Infantry with Burnside's Coast Division, Eighteenth Army Corps and Army of the James*. Milford, MA: King & Billings, 1884.

Denny, Joseph L. *Wearing the Blue with the Twenty-fifth Massachusetts Volunteer Infantry, with Burnside's Coast Division, Eighteenth Army Corps and Army of the James*. Worcester, MA: Putnam & Davis, 1879.

Derby, William P. *Bearing Arms in the Twenty-seventh Massachusetts Regiment of Volunteer Infantry During the Civil War, 1861–1865*. Boston, MA: Wright & Potter Printing Company, 1883.

Drake, J. Madison. *The History of the Ninth New Jersey Veteran Volunteers*. Elizabeth, NJ: Journal Printing House, 1889.

Draper, John G. *Recollections of a Varied Career*. Boston, MA: Little, Brown & Company, 1908.

Emilio, Luis F. *Roanoke Island: Its Occupation, Defense and Fall*. New York: Roanoke Associates, 1891.

Emmerton, James A. *A Record of the Twenty-third Regiment Massachusetts Volunteer Infantry in the War of the Rebellion, 1861–1865*. Boston, MA: William War & Company, 1886.

Everts, Hermann. *A Complete and Comprehensive History of the Ninth Regiment New Jersey Volunteer Infantry from Its First Organization to Its Final Muster-out*. Newark, NJ: A. Stephen Holbrook, 1865.

Gould, Joseph. *The Story of the Forty-eighth*. Philadelphia, PA: A.H.M. Slocum Company, 1908.

Graham, Matthew J. *The Ninth Regiment New York Volunteers (Hawkins's Zouaves), Being a History of the Regiment and Veteran Association from 1860 to 1900*. New York: self-published, 1900.

Green, Wharton J. *Recollections and Reflections: An Auto of Half a Century and More*. Raleigh, NC: Edwards and Broughton Printing Company, 1906.

Jackman, Lyman. *History of the Sixth New Hampshire Regiment in the War for the Union*. Concord, NH: Republican Press Association, 1891.

Johnson, Charles F. *The Long Roll*. East Aurora, NY: Roycrofters, 1911.

Johnson, Robert U., and Clarence C. Buell. *Battles and Leaders of the Civil War*. 4 vols. New York: Century Company, 1884–88.

Lincoln, Abraham. "Annual Message to Congress—Concluding Remarks." December 1, 1862. In *Collected Works of Abraham Lincoln*. Vol. 5. Edited by Roy P. Basler, Marion Dolores Pratt and Lloyd A. Dunlap. New Brunswick, NJ: Rutgers University Press, 1953, 537.

Loving, Jerome M., ed. *The Civil War Letters of George Washington Whitman*. Durham, NC: Duke University Press, 1975.

Moore, Frank, ed. *The Rebellion Record: A Diary of American Events, with Documents, Narratives, Illustrative Incidents, Poetry, etc*. 11 vols. plus supplement. New York: G.P. Putnam, 1861–68.

Parker, Thomas. *History of the Fifty-first Regiment of P.V. and V.V.* Philadelphia, PA: King and Baird, 1869.

Parker, William H. *Recollections of a Naval Officer, 1841–1865*. New York: Charles Scribner's Sons, 1883.

Parkhurst, V.P. *Proceedings of a Court of Inquiry in Regards to Reports Made by Major M.J. McCafferty and Others of Misconduct at the Battle of Roanoke Island February 8, 1862, by Captain V.P. Parkhurst, Company I Twenty-fifth Regiment, Massachusetts Volunteers*. Fitchburg, MA: Curtis and Bushnell, 1864.

Payne, Roger L. *Place Names of the Outer Banks*. Washington, NC: T.A. Williams, 1985.

Putnam, Samuel A. *The Story of Company A, Twenty-fifth Regiment, Massachusetts Volunteers in the War of the Rebellion*. Worcester, MA: Putnam, Davis & Company, 1886.

Roe, Alfred S. *The Twenty-fourth Regiment Massachusetts Volunteers, 1861–1865 "New England Guard Regiment."* Worcester, MA: Regimental Veteran Association, 1907.

Stone, James Madison. *Personal Recollections of the Civil War*. Boston, MA: self-published, 1918.

Traver, Lorenzo. "Burnside in North Carolina: Battles of Roanoke Island and Elizabeth City." *Personal Narratives of the Battles of the Rebellion, Being Papers Read Before the Rhode Island Soldiers and Sailors Historical Society* 2, no. 5 (1880).

United States Bureau of Census. *Population Schedules of the Eighth Census of the U.S. (1860)—Free Inhabitants of Currituck County, North Carolina*. Vol. 5. Washington, D.C.: Government Printing Office, 1860.

————. *Population Schedules of the Eighth Census of the U.S.—Slave Schedules of Currituck County, North Carolina.* Vol. 2. Washington, D.C.: Government Printing Office, 1860.

United States Naval War Records Office. *Official Records of the Union and Confederate Navies in the War of the Rebellion.* 30 vols. Washington, D.C.: Government Printing Office, 1894–1927.

United States Sanitary Commission. *Catalogue of the Museum of Flags, Trophies and Relics Relating to the Revolution, the War of 1812, the Mexican War, and the Present Rebellion.* New York: Charles O. Jones, 1864.

United States Senate. 37th Cong., 2nd sess. Executive Document 37. *Letter from Secretary of War Payne Answer to a Resolution of the Senate of the 30th Day of January, in Relation to the Vessels Purchased or Chartered for Use of the War Department Since the 1st Day of April Last.* Washington, D.C.: 1862.

United States War Department. *The War of the Rebellion: A Compilation of the Official Records of the Union and Confederate Armies.* 70 vols. in 128 parts. Washington, D.C.: Government Printing Office, 1880–1901.

Valentine, Herbert E. *The Story of Company F, 23d Massachusetts Volunteers in the War for the Preservation of the Union, 1861–1865.* Boston, MA: W.B. Clarke & Company, 1896.

Walcott, Charles F. *History of the Twenty-first Regiment Massachusetts Volunteers in the War for the Preservation of the Union, 1861–1865.* Boston, MA: Houghton, Mifflin and Company, 1882.

Welch, William L. "The Burnside Expedition, and Engagement at Roanoke Island." *Personal Narratives of the Battles of the Rebellion, Being Papers Read Before the Rhode Island Soldiers and Sailors Historical Society* 4, no. 9 (1890).

Whitney, John H.E. *The Hawkins Zouaves: (Ninth N.Y.V.) Their Battles and Marches.* New York: self-published, 1866.

Wise, John S. *The End of an Era.* Boston, MA: Houghton, Mifflin, 1902.

Woodbury, Augustus. *Major General Ambrose E. Burnside and the Ninth Army Corps.* Providence, RI: Sidney S. Rider & Brother, 1867.

# SECONDARY

Abbott, John S.C. "Heroic Deeds of Heroic Men." *Harper's New Monthly Magazine* 34, no. 18 (1867): 559–71.

Alduino, Frank W., and David J. Coles. *Sons of Garibaldi in Blue and Gray: Italians in the American Civil War.* Youngstown, NY: Cambria Press, 2007.

Allen, Thomas B. *Harriet Tubman, Secret Agent: How Daring Slaves and Free Blacks Spied for the Union During the Civil War*. Washington, D.C.: National Geographic, 2006.

Andrews, J. Cutler. *The North Reports the Civil War*. Pittsburgh, PA: University of Pittsburgh Press, 1955.

Bancroft, Frederic. *The Life of William H. Seward*. 2 vols. New York: Harper & Brothers Publishers, 1900.

Barrett, John G. *The Civil War in North Carolina*. Chapel Hill: University of North Carolina Press, 1963.

Bassett, John Spencer. *Slavery in the State of North Carolina*. Baltimore, MD: Johns Hopkins University Press, 1899.

Birdsong, James C. *Brief Sketches of the North Carolina State Troops in the War Between the States*. Raleigh, NC: Edwards & Broughton, 1894.

Bridges, Hal. *Lee's Maverick General*. Lincoln: University of Nebraska Press, 1991.

Burlingame, Michael. *Abraham Lincoln: A Life*. 2 vols. Baltimore, MD: Johns Hopkins University Press, 2008.

———. *The Inner World of Abraham Lincoln*. Champaign: University of Illinois Press, 1994.

Clark, Walter. *Histories of the Several Regiments and Battalions from North Carolina in the Great War 1861–'65*. Vol. 2. Goldsboro, NC: Nash Brothers, 1901.

Click, Patricia. *Time Full of Trial*. Chapel Hill: University of North Carolina Press, 2001.

Croffut, W.A., and John M. Morris. *The Military History of Connecticut During the War of 1861–65*. New York: Ledyard Bill, 1868.

Cullen, Joseph P. "The Very Beau Ideal of a Soldier: A Personality Profile of Ambrose E. Burnside." *Civil War Times Illustrated* 16, no. 5 (August 1977).

Cutchins, John Abram. *A Famous Command: The Richmond Light Infantry Blues*. Richmond, VA: Garret and Massie, 1934.

Daley, Robert W. "Burnside's Amphibious Division." In *Assault from the Sea: Essays on the History of Amphibious Warfare*. Edited by Merrill L. Bartlett. Annapolis, MD: Naval Institute Press, 1983.

Davis, John. "Up the Beach and Into Battle." Edited by William Adams. *Civil War Times Illustrated* 25, no. 6 (October 1986): 33–34.

Davis, William C. *Battle at Bull Run: A History of the First Major Campaign of the Civil War*. Garden City, NY: Doubleday and Company Incorporated, 1997.

Edmonds, Thomas F. "Operations in North Carolina, 1861–1862." *Operations on the Atlantic Coast, 1861–1865*. Vol. 9. *Papers of the Military Historical Society of Massachusetts*. Boston, MA: 1912.

Ellis, Edward S. *The History of Our Country: From the Discovery of America to the Present Time*. 8 vols. Cincinnati, OH: Jones Brothers, 1900.

Foote, Shelby. *The Civil War: A Narrative: Fort Sumter to Perryville*. New York: Vintage Books, 1986.

Goodwin, Doris Kearns. *Team of Rivals: The Political Genius of Abraham Lincoln*. New York: Simon & Schuster, 2005.

Harper, Raymond L. *A History of Chesapeake*. Charleston, SC: The History Press, 2007.

Hill, Daniel H., Jr. *North Carolina in the War Between the States, Bethel to Sharpsburg*. 2 vols. Raleigh, NC: Edwards and Broughton Company, 1926.

Hinds, John W. *Invasion and Conquest of North Carolina: Anatomy of a Gunboat War*. Shippensburg, PA: Burd Street Press, 1998.

Jones, William. "Britain's Surrogate War Against the Union, 1861–65." Schiller Institute. http://schillerinstitute.org/strategic/2011/us_civil_war.html.

Jordan, Weymouth T., and Louis H. Manarin. *North Carolina Troops, 1861–1865: A Roster*. 14 vols. Raleigh: North Carolina Division of Archives and History, 1966.

Linn, William Alexander. *Horace Greeley: Founder and Editor of the New York Tribune*. New York: Appleton and Company, 1912.

Long, Mary Wood. *The Five Lost Colonies of Dare*. Elizabeth City: Family Research Society of Northeastern North Carolina, 2000.

Marvel, William. *Burnside*. Chapel Hill: University of North Carolina Press, 1991.

McConnell, William F. *Remember Reno*. Shippensburg, PA: White Mane Publishing, 1996.

Naylor, Colin T., Jr. *Civil War Days in a Country Village*. Peekskill, NY: Highland Press, 1961.

Owens, Margaret Dawson. "The Confederate Flag." In *Pasquotank Historical Society Year Book, 1955–1957*. Vol. 2. Edited by John Elliot Wood. Elizabeth City, NC: Pell Paper Box Company, 1957.

Poore, Benjamin Perley. *The Life and Public Services of Ambrose E. Burnside*. Providence, RI: J.A. & R.A. Reid, 1882.

Post, Lydia Minturn. *Soldiers' Letters, from Camps, Battlefield and Prison*. New York: Bunce & Huntington, 1865.

Powell, William S. *North Carolina Through Four Centuries*. Chapel Hill: University of North Carolina Press, 1989.

Sauers, Richard. *A Succession of Honorable Victories: The Burnside Expedition in North Carolina*. Dayton, OH: Morningside Press, 1996.

Sauers, Richard, ed. *The Civil War Journal of Colonel Bolton Fifty-first Pennsylvania: August 20, 1861–August 2, 1865.* Conshoken, PA: Combined Publishing, 2000.

Scharf, Thomas. *History of the Confederate States Navy from Its Organization to the Surrender of Its Last Vessel.* 2 vols. New York: Rogers & Sherwood, 1887.

Siegel, Steven. "British Foreign Policy During the American Civil War: January 1860 to September 1862." Canton, MA: Concord Review, 2005. http://www.tcr.org/tcr/essays/eprize07_Civil%20War%20Diplomacy%2016_1.pdf.

Stick, David. *The Outer Banks of North Carolina.* Chapel Hill: University of North Carolina Press, 1958.

Stillwell, Margaret Bingham. "General Hawkins as He Revealed Himself to His Librarian." In *The Papers of the Bibliographical Society of America, Part II.* 16 vols. Chicago: University of Chicago Press 1922.

Troiani, Don, Earl J. Coates and Michael J. McAfee. *Don Troiani's Regiments & Uniforms of the Civil War.* Mechanicsburg, PA: Stackpole Books, 2002.

Trotter, William R. *Ironclads and Columbiads: The Civil War in North Carolina: The Coast.* Winston-Salem, NC: John F. Blair, 1989.

Virginia National Guard. *160th Anniversary, Richmond Light Infantry Blues: 176th Combat Team, VANG, 178–1949.* Richmond: Virginia National Guard, 1949.

Wheeler, Gerald E., and A. Stuart Pitt. "The Fifty-third New York: A Zoo-Zoo Tale." *New York History* 37 (1956): 414–31.

Wise, Barton H. *The Life of Henry A. Wise of Virginia, 1806–1876.* New York: Macmillan Company, 1899.

# NEWSPAPERS

*Brooklyn (NY) Daily Eagle*
*Burlington (VT) Free Press*
*Chelsea (MA) Telegraph and Pioneer*
*Fort Worth (TX) Gazette.*
*Frank Leslie's Illustrated Newspaper (NY)*
*Gallipolis (OH) Journal*
*Geneva (NY) Courier*
*Harper's Weekly*
*Holmes County (OH) Republican*
*Illustrated London News*

*Iola (KS) Register*
*Lafayette (LA) Gazette*
*Lewiston (ME) Evening Journal*
*Macon (GA) Daily Telegraph*
*Memphis (TN) Daily Appeal*
*(Washington, D.C.) National Republican*
*(Washington, D.C.) National Tribune*
*New York Daily Tribune*
*New York Evening Express*
*New York Evening Post*

*New York Herald*

*New York Illustrated News*

*New York Sun*

*New York Times*

*New York World*

*Philadelphia Inquirer*

*Philadelphia Press*

*Putnam County (GA) Countryman*

*Raleigh (NC) Weekly Standard*

*Randolph (MA) Transcript*

*Richmond (VA) Daily Dispatch*

*Richmond (VA) Day Book*

*Richmond (VA) Examiner*

*Richmond (VA) Times-Dispatch*

*Roxbury (MA) City Gazette*

*Stamford (CT) Advocate*

*Stauton (VA) Spectator*

*(Battleboro) Vermont Phoenix*

## ORIGINAL PAPERS

National Archives. John Henry Byrd, Ninth New York. Pension. Washington D.C.

————. John William Pattison, Ninth New York. Pension. Washington D.C.

University of California. George Hollis Papers. "Battle of Roanoke Island." San Diego Library. San Diego, CA.

# Index

# About the Author

Michael P. Zatarga grew up surrounded by history in New York's Hudson Valley. This led to a career in the history field, first with a BA from State University of New York at New Paltz, then an MA from Western Connecticut State University and then work with the National Park Service at Guilford Courthouse NMP in Greensboro, North Carolina, and Fort Raleigh NHS in Manteo, North Carolina. Michael has been involved in living history since high school and has spoken at activities from Massachusetts to South Carolina. He was the living  history coordinator for the 150th Anniversary Commemoration of the Civil War on the "Outer Banks: Flags Over Hatters" event. He has written several articles, including the National Park Service's informational brochure on the Battle of Roanoke Island. He lives on Roanoke Island with his wife and three children.

*Visit us at*
www.historypress.net

·················································

*This title is also available as an e-book*